Carrier Fleets

Flat Top Fleets – Drones at Sea – Naval Aviation – Carri

LEFT: China how has two carriers in frontline service and a third is undergoing sea trials. (PEOPLE'S LIBERATION ARMY NAVY)

FAR LEFT: The F-35B Lightning II is now replacing the AV-8B Harrier jump jet in navies that operate smaller aircraft carriers. (MOD/CROWN COPYRIGHT)

LEFT: NATO's carrier strike force out to sea during Exercise Steadfast Defender in January and February 2024. (MOD/CROWN COPYRIGHT)

LEFT: Unmanned aerial vehicles or drones are now starting to appear on the decks of aircraft carriers of a number of navies. (US NAVY)

ISBN: 978 1 80282 985 3
Editor: Tim Ripley
Data and photo research: Fergus Ripley
Senior editor, specials: Roger Mortimer
Email: roger.mortimer@keypublishing.com
Production editor: Paul Sander
Cover Design: Steve Donovan
Design: SJmagic DESIGN SERVICES, India
Advertising Sales Manager:
Sam Clark
Email: sam.clark@keypublishing.com
Tel: 01780 755131

Advertising Production: Becky Antoniades
Email: Rebecca.antoniades@keypublishing.com

SUBSCRIPTION/MAIL ORDER
Key Publishing Ltd, PO Box 300, Stamford, Lincs, PE9 1NA
Tel: 01780 480404
Subscriptions email: subs@keypublishing.com
Mail Order email: orders@keypublishing.com
Website: www.keypublishing.com/shop

PUBLISHING
Group CEO and Publisher: Adrian Cox

Published by
Key Publishing Ltd, PO Box 100, Stamford, Lincs, PE9 1XQ
Tel: 01780 755131 **Website:** www.keypublishing.com

PRINTING
Precision Colour Printing Ltd, Haldane,
Halesfield 1, Telford, Shropshire. TF7 4QQ

DISTRIBUTION
Seymour Distribution Ltd, 2 Poultry Avenue, London,
EC1A 9PU
Enquiries Line: 02074 294000.

Photo Credits: The author has attempted, where possible, to credit the originators of all the images used in this publication. Any errors will be corrected in future editions.

Carrier Fleets 2024

Flat Tops of the World

Aircraft carriers are powerful weapons of war that have dominated naval warfare since the early days of World War Two.

When the first aircraft successfully took off from a warship in November 1910 little could those pioneering naval aviators could have realised that three decades later the aircraft carrier would be the dominant weapon in naval warfare.

Britain, Japan and the United States used aircraft carriers aggressively in World War Two and transformed sea battles. No longer did fleets have to sail within sight of their opponents to secure victory at sea.

The dramatic strike at Taranto in November 1940 by the Royal Navy and then the devastating surprise Japanese attack on the US Pacific Fleet at Pearl Harbor in December 1941 appeared to render battleships obsolete overnight.

Over the next four years, aircraft carriers dominated the war in the Pacific and the decisive tipping point in the war was the Battle of Midway in 1942 that crippled Japan's carrier fleet. It never recovered.

RIGHT: Putting 'jets in the air' is what carrier operations are all about, to take the fight to the enemy and protect the fleet. (US NAVY)

BELOW: Aircraft carriers are floating airfields that can operate anywhere on the high seas to bring airpower to bear in time of crisis or war. (MOD/CROWN COPYRIGHT)

In the Cold War carriers became essential for crisis response missions. For generations, US Presidents have asked the same question famously attributed to the 41st US President, George HW Bush, who said the first question he always asked when a crisis erupted, "Where are our aircraft carriers?"

Modern aircraft carriers have capabilities far in advance of those available to the pioneers of naval aviation 100 years ago. Today aircraft carriers can launch squadrons of supersonic stealth fighters, have flight decks full of anti submarine helicopters and airborne early warning aircraft, as well as magazines full of precision guided missiles. The United States and France have nuclear powered aircraft carriers that can sail on patrol for months at a time, without having to put into port to refuel.

These aircraft carriers can dominate huge areas of sea and project air power over vast distances. The essential feature of a modern aircraft carrier is a large flight deck that can launch and recover fast jet combat aircraft. These have long been nicknamed 'flat tops' for obvious reasons. Modern carriers are now so big and carry so many aircraft that they are often dubbed 'super carriers' to differentiate them from the carriers of World War Two vintage. The USS *Hornet* that launched Colonel Jimmy Doolittle's raiders to attack Tokyo in April 1942 came in at 20,000 tons. This is now dwarfed by the most recent US navy carrier, the USS *Gerald R Ford*, which has a displacement of more than 100,000 tons.

In *Carrier Fleets 2024* we describe the world's aircraft carrier fleets, looking at which navies have flat tops and their plans to build more of these monster ships. Today, there are three main types of aircraft carriers. Strike carriers are optimised to attack targets ashore with waves of attack jets. Anti-submarine or sea control carriers are optimised to dominate sea zones, both above and below the water. Flat top amphibious assault ships are built to project contingents of marines ashore by helicopter and landing craft, supported by jump jets operating from them.

As well as looking at the world's carriers and the aircraft squadrons that fly off them, we will also describe how navies use them in their battle plans and national defence strategies.

Recent combat operations in the Red Sea involving flat tops will also be examined to find pointers to the future of flat top aviation.

An increasing number of navies want to add carriers to their fleets, despite their huge cost. USS *Gerald R Ford* cost $12.8 billion, which is more than many countries annual defence budgets. Ten navies currently operate 35 carriers and seven more carriers are under construction, with seven more planned. The prestige and combat power of aircraft carriers is still in high demand.

Tim Ripley
Editor
June 2024

LEFT: Carrier power. The US Naval Base at San Diego is home to the US Pacific Fleet's aircraft carriers, with USS *Ronald Reagan*, USS *Carl Vinson* and USS *Nimitz* being seen here. (US NAVY)

BELOW LEFT: The USS *Midway* is preserved at Naval Base Point Loma, near San Diego, as tribute to the sailors and naval aviators who fought in the 1942 battle that she is named after, as well generations of US Navy personnel who served on the ship between 1945 and 1992. (US NAVY)

BELOW: Tim Ripley inspects HMS *Prince of Wales* during her construction at Rosyth in 2017. (TIM RIPLEY)

Carrier Battles through the Ages

Naval Airpower Dominates

RIGHT: Japan's dramatic surprise strike against the US fleet at Pearl Harbor in December 1941 changed the balance of power in the Pacific and demonstrated that the aircraft carrier was now the dominant naval weapon of war.
(US NATIONAL ARCHIVES)

The first recorded combat action involving carrier launch aircraft took place in July 1918, when British aircraft took off from the converted cruiser HMS *Furious* to attack a German Zepplin base at Tønder on the German-Danish border. Seven Sopwith Camels took off to attack the airship sheds at the base and dropped bombs on it, setting two Zepplins on fire.

The mission was a one-way trip. HMS *Furious* could only launch aircraft from a platform mounted on top of its forward deck. There was no way for pilots to land back on the ship. One aircraft had to ditch soon after launch due to mechanical problems. Out of the six aircraft that attacked the target, three were short of fuel and landed in nearby neutral

BELOW: For the rest of the Pacific war, the US and Japanese navies tried to sink their opponent's aircraft carriers to win air supremacy at sea.
(US NATIONAL ARCHIVES)

Denmark. The pilots were interned for the rest of the war. The remaining three aircraft headed back to British fleet. Two of the pilots managed to find their way back and ditched their aircraft alongside the British warships and were successful recovered. One pilot was never heard of again and is presumed to have run out of fuel and ditched.

After this early beginning, navies around the world saw the potential and by the start of World War Two the first 'proper' aircraft carriers, with full length flight decks that could launch and recover aircraft, were in frontline service.

The British Royal Navy lost two aircraft carriers to German submarines and battleships in the first nine months of World War Two. Poor tactics and decisions were blamed for the loss of the ships. By November 1940, the Royal Navy commander in the Mediterranean, Admiral Andrew Cunningham, came up with a daring plan to make a rapid dash with his carrier, HMS *Illustrious*, towards the Italian fleet's anchorage at Taranto. In a night-time attack, 21 Fairy Swordfish aircraft launched torpedoes against the Italian warships. For the loss of two aircraft, the Fleet Air Arm strike force badly damaged the three most powerful Italian battleships. It changed the naval balance in the Mediterranean.

At the same time, the Japanese Imperial Navy was working on similar plans to strike at the US Pacific Fleet at Pearl Harbor in the Hawaiian Islands. The infamous attack on December 7, 1941, transformed naval warfare. When 353 Japanese aircraft surprised the American fleet, they managed to sink four battleships

and damage nine other warships, as well as destroying 188 aircraft and damaging 159 more. The US air and naval defences were caught completely by surprise. Only 29 Japanese aircraft were lost and 74 more were slightly damaged during the attack.

The attacks at Taranto and Pearl Harbour became the classic examples of ship-to-shore strike missions, which devastated land targets. This involved carrier fleets moving covertly into range of their targets and launching attack waves before the enemy has

time to react. The US struck back when B-25 bombers launched from the USS *Hornet* struck at Tokyo in April 1942.

Both the Japanese and American naval commands quickly decided that the route to victory was through sinking the enemy's carriers. During the Battles of Coral Sea in May 1942 and the Battle of Midway the following month, the rival fleets manoeuvred for advantage. Aircraft carriers launched attack waves of torpedo and dive bombers to find the opposing carriers. The aircraft »

ABOVE: The Battle of Midway in June 1942 changed the course of the Pacific war, when the US Navy managed to sink all four of the carriers the Japanese committed to the action. (US NATIONAL ARCHIVES)

BELOW: The US Navy perfected the tactics and technology of aircraft carrier operations during the Pacific campaign that defeated Imperial Japan. (US NATIONAL ARCHIVES)

Independence-class light carriers and 77 escort carriers.

As US Marine Corps amphibious forces advanced across the Pacific in their 'island-hopping' campaign to capture key islands until American forces were within striking distance of the Japanese home islands. The US Navy protected this campaign with huge fleets of aircraft carriers. Their aircraft hunted for Japanese warships threatening the American fleet and shot down any enemy aircraft that approached. Once the US Marines stormed ashore, carrier-borne aircraft bombed Japanese troop positions to clear the way for the assault troops to advance.

US aircraft carriers were floating airfields that allows American airpower to operate far from airbases and bring the war to the shores of Japan. This was the use of carrier airpower for power projections on a massive scale.

In 1950, US and British aircraft carriers found themselves on the frontline of the Cold War when Communist troops invaded South Korea. US and allied troops found themselves under pressure and retreated to a small bridgehead in the southern tip of the Korean peninsula. To try to bring airpower to bear to slow the Communist advance, the US Navy and Royal Navy dispatched their carriers at full speed to the coast of Korea. They then launched their

ABOVE: When the US Navy built a new generation of 'super carriers' in the 1950s and 1960s, it reinforced its naval dominance in the Cold War confrontation with the Soviet Union. (US NAVY)

BELOW: Three of the six aircraft carriers massed by the US Navy of the 1991 Gulf War. (US NAVY)

patrolled over hundreds of miles to find their targets. The strike force that found the enemy carriers first invariably won the battle.

At Coral Sea, honours were even with each side losing one carrier. The following month, the Americans turned the tables on the Japanese by sinking four carriers for the loss of one of their own. After this defeat,

the Japanese carrier fleet never recovered and were on the defensive for the remainder of the Pacific campaign.

US industrial might now started to kick into gear, with carrier production ramping up to a rate that the Japanese could not rival. Over the next four years the Americans built seventeen Essex-class fleet carriers, eleven

ABOVE: The F-14 Tomcat was the iconic US Navy carrier fighter from 1974 to 2006 and stared the 1986 movie *Top Gun*, with Tom Cruise. (US NAVY)

aircraft to strike at North Korean columns. Aircraft carriers proved an ideal platform to use air power to influence events in scenarios where land-based aircraft were out of range.

Escalating tension in South East Asia in the early 1960s prompted the United States Navy to dispatch aircraft carriers to the Gulf of Tonkin, off the coast of North Vietnam. As Communist attacks on South Vietnam escalated, the US responded with a series of air strikes launched from its carriers against North Vietnam. This era cemented the place of the aircraft carrier in modern US military strategy as America's '9/11 emergency force'.

American aircraft carriers have played important roles in almost every US military intervention since the Vietnam War, but other nations have seen the value of naval aviation.

India's aircraft carrier, the INS *Vikrant* launched air strikes against land targets during the 1971 Indo-Pakistan war. As a result, India has continued to invest in carrier airpower.

The 1982 Falklands war between Britain and Argentina proved to be the only occasion since World War Two where rival carrier battle groups duelled against each other in a shooting war. This war demonstrated again that control of the air was decisive in naval warfare.

In the post-Cold War era, a number of nations have used their aircraft carriers as power projection platforms, supporting humanitarian interventions and non-combat evacuation operations on several occasions. Most prominently, the FS *Charles de Gaulle* operated as a strike carrier during the NATO interventions in Afghanistan after 2001 and again in Libya in 2011. Jets from the nuclear-powered carrier also attacked Islamic State-linked targets in Syria and Iraq in 2015 and 2016. Russia's only aircraft carrier, the RFS *Admiral Kuznetsov* launched its jets into action over Syria in 2016.

New entrants into the carrier game have been keen to demonstrate their new-found military power. The Chinese People's Liberation Army Navy (PLAN) has launched a rapid programme to build aircraft carriers. Beijing's navy has recently used them in a series of naval war games off Taiwan in a bid to intimidate the island state.

The aircraft carrier has proved to be an adaptable tool of naval strategy in both peace and war. Critics of aircraft carriers claim they are expensive military relics with little relevance in the age of drones and hypersonic missiles. The central role played by aircraft carriers in several recent military operations suggests that reports of their demise might be premature.

LEFT: On Yankee Station. The US Navy's aircraft carriers played a key role in the air war against Vietnam between 1964 and 1975. (US NATIONAL ARCHIVES)

Modern Carrier Fleets

Airpower at Sea in 21st Century

Aircraft carriers have always operated as part of battle groups with other warships, submarines and support vessels. They provide force protect for the carrier and also help in the hunt for targets for ship-borne aircraft to strike at.

Modern day carrier battle groups continue this tradition, but they incorporate the latest technology – intelligence feed from drones, satellite communications, anti-ballistic missile defences and precision guided weapons.

The aircraft carrier is at the heart of the modern naval battlegroup, providing a floating airfield to launch and recover strike, reconnaissance, airborne early warning, anti-submarine and air defence aircraft. A carrier's air wing, or air group, is its main offensive element, projecting air power ashore against land targets or against an enemy's fleet. This is the key business of the aircraft carrier. It is an offensive weapon of war and getting the ship into position to strike at the enemy is the key task of its commanders.

In World War Two, carrier air groups struck at the enemy with torpedo bombers and dive bombers. Today, more modern guided weapons are the main offensive systems available to naval aviators. Satellite and laser guided bombs and missiles allow a handful of naval aircraft to inflict heavy damage on land targets. Anti-radiation missiles also allow carrier-borne aircraft to neutralise enemy air defences. To defeat enemy warships, sea skimming anti-ship missiles are the main air launched weapon of carrier air groups.

Land attack missiles, such as the US Tomahawk, fired from destroyers and submarines provide battle group commanders with further strike options, particularly against heavily defended targets. They can be used

THE WORLD'S AIRCRAFT CARRIERS IN 2024			
Navy	**In Service**	**In Build**	**Proposed**
China People's Liberation Army Navy			
Type 001/Kuznetsov-class	1		
Type 002/Kuznetsov-class	1		
Type 003/Fujian-class		1	
Type 004-class		1	
French Navy			
Charles de Gaulle-class	1		
PANG-class			1
Indian Navy			
Modified Kiev-class	1		
Vikrant-class	1		1
IAC3-class			1
Italian Navy			
Cavour-class	1		
Giuseppe Garibaldi-class	1		
Trieste-class	1		
Japanese Maritime Self Defence Force			
Izumo-class	2		
Russian Navy			
Admiral Kuznetsov-class 1	1		1
Spanish Navy			
Juan Carlos I-class	1		
Turkish Navy			
Juan Carlos I-class	1		
Future Carrier			1
US Navy			
Nimitz-class	10		
Gerald R Ford-class	1	3	1
Wasp-class	7		
America-class	2	2	1
Royal Navy			
Queen Elizabeth-class	2		

by themselves or to hit air defence sites to open the way for manned aircraft to penetrate to their targets. Several nations are experimenting with launching drones from aircraft carriers to expand the options open to battle group commanders in complex battle scenarios.

Fighter jets and airborne early warning aircraft launched from a carrier also provide an air defence shield for the fleet. The importance airborne early warning has risen dramatically in the era of sea skimming anti-ship missiles. Only by elevating a radar high into the sky on an aircraft or helicopter can the effect of the curvature of the earth be overcome, to give effective early warning of inbound sea skimming missiles.

Aircraft carriers have long been used as command-and-control centres with the battlegroup commanders and their staff embarked onboard. In World War Two, orders and messages were sent by unreliable radios or even signal flags when battlegroups were maintaining radio silence. Today, naval commanders control their fleets via computerised data networks that transmit information instantly over high capacity and encrypted radio links. Tactical information such as radar tracks and signals intelligence are displayed on electronic maps that are automatically updated in the real time. These provide commanders with a 'god's eye view' of the tactical situation over thousands of miles of sea and air space. They are known as air or surface 'operational pictures' and show the position of every friendly or hostile vessel and aircraft, as well civilian merchant vessels and airliners.

As a result, modern day naval commanders have an unprecedented view of what is happening around their battlegroups. Not since the days of Nelson, when the famous British admiral could see everyone of his ships from this flag ship have naval commanders had so much understanding of naval battles.

The laws of physics intervene in the creation and maintenance of operation pictures because data networks are only as good as the range of the radio systems they flow across. Carrier launched airborne early warning aircraft play a key role in establishing these networks by acting as communications hubs, and

receiving data over long distances by overcoming the curvature of the air. Not surprisingly, often the first aircraft to launch from a carrier during active operations is the airborne early warning aircraft to extend radar coverage over the horizon and expand the battle groups communications network. The most reassuring message any naval aviator can receive is 'picture clear' from radar operators who are signalling that there are no enemy aircraft or other threats in the vicinity.

Protecting the aircraft carrier from enemy warships and submarines is the job of the surface action group of frigates and destroyers. These throw a layered defensive ring around the »

ABOVE LEFT: Britain's HMS *Prince of Wales* **led the NATO carrier task force during Exercise Steadfast Defender to rehearse keeping open sea lines in North Atlantic.** (MOD/CROWN COPYRIGHT)

LEFT: The arrival of the 5th generation F-35 Lightning on the decks of US, British, Italian and Japanese flat tops is transforming western carrier aviation. (MOD/CROWN COPYRIGHT)

carrier to look for enemy warships and neutralise any threats. Anti-submarine helicopters embarked on these warships extend the protective ring under water to keep enemy submarines at bay.

Destroyers provide an additional layer of air defence to back up carrier launched fighters with surface-to-air missiles. The US RIM-161 Standard missile and the European Aster missile can hit inbound enemy aircraft or drones dozens of kilometres away from the battle group and can also engage enemy ballistic missiles as they drop from space.

Modern technology has transformed how aircraft carriers can be used in battle, but they remain crucially dependent on reliable and effective re-supply at sea to ensure they remain combat ready. In the great naval battles of the Pacific war, the US Navy developed the concept of a 'fleet train' of supply ships that would follow its carriers. These specially modified ships were fitted with equipment to pass fuel, ammunition, food and fresh water to replenish carriers at sea after battles. This meant US aircraft carriers could stay at sea for prolonged periods without having to return to port to refuel and rearm.

The modern-day carrier battle group has its own fleet train of tankers and supply ships to keep it fighting. Fuel lines and cargo hoists are passed over to the carrier from the supply ships so they can replenish it far out at sea. Nuclear-powered carriers do not need to refuel for years at a time but its air wing can only keep flying and fighting if it has aviation fuel, bombs and missiles. The carrier's crew also need to be fed to keep fighting, so food is an essential ingredient of its combat capability. Replenishment at sea is not very glamorous but it is a key element of fielding and effective aircraft capability with a global reach.

In the 21st century, real-time satellite surveillance of naval movements is now available to many nations which has greatly complicated aircraft carrier operations. It is now almost impossible for aircraft carriers to 'disappear' for weeks at a time in the expanse of the world oceans. Pearl Harbor style surprise attacks may be impossible in the future, but navies are looking at new ways to reduce the vulnerability of the carriers to modern precision guided missiles or drones.

Electronic war jamming to neutralise the control frequencies or guidance systems of missiles and drones are now 'must have' items of

equipment. Laser weapons are also being explored as a way to increase the defensive power of carrier battle groups.

There have been many predictions that drones would replace manned aircraft, but this will not necessarily spell the end of the aircraft carrier.

Drones still need runways to launch and recover them, as well as hanger decks to store and prepare them for action. Ships with a large flat deck will still be needed even, if the aircraft they launch might not contain human crews. The sun has not yet set on the aircraft carrier.

ABOVE: The F/A-18 Hornet and Super Hornet has been the standard strike fighter on the decks of US Navy carriers for almost 20 years and the new F-35C Lightning II is starting to join them. (US NAVY)

BELOW: RAF and Royal Navy F-35B Lightning jets are the core of the air group on Britain's new generation of aircraft carriers. (MOD/CROWN COPYRIGHT)

Battle of the MAB

Carrier Action – Red Sea 2023–24

RIGHT: F/A-18E/F Super Hornets based on the USS *Dwight D Eisenhower* led air strikes against Houthi missile and drone batteries firing on commercial shipping in the Red Sea. (US NAVY)

RIGHT: The Pentagon named the mission to protect Red Sea shipping, Operation Prosperity Guardian. (US NAVY)

BELOW: The USS *Dwight D Eisenhower* arrived in the Red Sea in December 2023 o join Operation Prosperity Guardian. (US NAVY)

When Hamas fighters breached Israel's border wall around the Gaza Strip on October 7, 2023, it set off a chain of events that rapidly escalated into a conflict that spread across the Middle East. The following day, US President Joe Biden ordered the USS *Gerald R Ford* carrier strike group to sail for the Eastern Mediterranean. Days later she was joined by the USS *Dwight D Eisenhower* as a show of force to deter other regional powers getting involved in the Gaza war.

Houthi rebels in Yemen declared their support for the Palestinians and said they would attack any Israeli ships in the Red Sea. On October 19, 2023, USS *Carney* on patrol off Yemen shot down four cruise missiles and 15 drones over a period of nine hours. Within weeks, attacks on merchant shipping in the Red Sea were happening on a daily basis. One ship was captured by Houthi commandos who landed by helicopter.

US Central Command now decided to reinforce its naval patrols in the Red Sea and dispatched the USS *Bataan* Amphibious Ready Group, as well as other warships, to uphold freedom of navigation. The amphibious assault ship stayed on station in the centre of the Red Sea for two months, with its US Marine Corps Bell AH-1Y Cobra

attack helicopters and McDonnell Douglas AV-8B Harrier II jump jets flying patrols to deter Houthi attacks. A series of engagement zones were set up down the Red Sea so Houthi missiles and drones could be rapidly

intercepted. One AV-8B pilot was credited with intercepting seven Houthi drones, although it is not cle if he shot down the drones or caused them to miss their targets.

Captain Earl Ehrhart of Marine Attack Squadron 231 (VMA-231), the "Ace of Spades," told the BBC in an interview, "We took a Harrier jet and modified it for air defence, we loade it up with missiles and that way were able to respond to their drone attacks."

The USS *Bataan* stayed on station i the Red Sea as Houthi attacks steadi escalated, prompting the United States to launch Operation Prosperit Guardian to better co-ordinate international naval forces in the region. Iranian backed-militia group across the Iraq and Syria had also

stepped-up drone and rocket attacks on US bases in these countries. To deter further escalation, the US Navy dispatched the USS *Dwight D Eisenhower* to the Arabian Gulf to launch her jets on combat air patrols over Iraq and Syria.

After the USS *Bataan* Amphibious Ready Group sailed north through the Suez Canal on December 28, she was replaced in the Red Sea by the USS *Dwight D Eisenhower*. Even before the carrier passed through the Bab al-Mandeb (BAM) Straits into the Red Sea, her air group was in action. As she sailed through the Gulf of Aden on December 26, a Boeing F/A-18E/F Super Hornet of Navy Strike Fighter Squadron (VFA)105 were launched to help protect the US Navy destroyer, USS *Laboon*, as she patrolled the Red Sea. During the 10 hour-long engagement, twelve one-way attack drones, three anti-ship ballistic missiles, and two land attack cruise missiles were shot down, including one drone which was destroyed by AIM-9X Block II Sidewinder missile, in the first ever air-to-air kill for the weapon.

On the carrier's first day in the Red Sea, Sikorsky HM-60R Seahawk armed helicopters of Helicopter Maritime Strike (HMS) 74 intercepted and sunk three Houthi patrol boats, which were detected attempting to put a boarding party on a cargo vessel.

The presence of the carrier, as well as her support cruiser and destroyers, in the Red Sea dramatically increased the firepower available to Operation Prosperity Guardian. The 'Ike' took up station in the centre of the Red Sea and began launching her Super Hornets on combat air patrols over the fleet. Her Grumman E-2D Hawkeye airborne early warning (AEW) aircraft were present around the clock to monitor Houthi threats. The radar picture

LEFT: During November and December 2023, AV-8B Harrier II jump jets flying off the USS Bataan provided air cover for coalition naval forces in the Red Sea. (US NAVY)

LEFT: Houthi attacks in Red Sea continued during 2024. US and coalition warships offered assistance and helped the crew of MV *True Confidence* deal with the aftermath of ballistic anti-ship missile strike. (US NAVY)

BELOW: The USS *Dwight D Eisenhower* entered the Red Sea at the end of December 2023 to lead the coalition naval operation against Houthi forces based in Yemen. (US NAVY)

collected by the E-2Ds, of Navy Airborne Command and Control Squadron (VAW) 123, was shared by real time data links with all coalition warships in the Red Sea and Gulf of Aden, as well as the US Air Force-led Combined Air Operations Centre at Al Udeid Airbase in Qatar, which controlled all allied air operations in the Middle East.

A massive wave of Houthi missiles and drones was launched on January 9, 2024, in an incident that became known as the 'Battle of the BAM Strait'. By the time the attack was over, US and British forces had shot down 18 of 21 Houthi weapons. Super Hornets of VFA-105 claimed two more air-to-air kills with AIM-9X missiles. »

President Biden now ordered the US Navy to strike back against the Houthi missile and drone launch sites, as well their airfields and command posts. The USS *Dwight D Eisenhower* was tasked to lead the strikes, which were scheduled to kick off on January 12. VFA-105 led the strikes. More than 150 munitions dropped by US Navy Super Hornets and British Eurofighter Typhoon jets, as well as US Navy Tomahawk land attack missiles, struck 28 locations within Houthi-controlled areas. As the Super Hornets approached their targets, they launched two AGM-88G Advanced Anti-Radiation Guided Missiles (AARGM) to suppress Houthi air defences.

Houthi resistance only seemed to escalate, and more attacks were launched against shipping in the Red Sea. Jets from the USS *Dwight D Eisenhower* continued their air patrols and on January 14, Super Hornets scored another first when they shot down a Houthi cruise missile heading towards USS *Laboon*. Other jets were launched as snap strikes against drone and missile launchers that were spotted moving into firing positions. Pairs of Super Hornets were kept 'up and ready' on the deck of the Ike, ready to launch as soon as intelligence of Houthi activity was detected.

US Naval aviators had to rapidly adapt to the Houthi's unconventional attacks tactics, with the Boeing F/A-18G Growlers of Electronic Attack Squadron (VAQ) 130 flying daily patrols to detect missile launches and pass warning to coalition ships.

In another bid to put a lid on the crisis, two days later another large wave of US and British air strikes were launched on targets across Yemen. This time, VFA-32 led the strike. There were two more large US-British strikes over the next month. Up to February 15, the Ike's carrier strike group — which includes the cruiser USS *Philippine Sea*, the destroyers USS *Mason*, USS *Gravely*, USS *Laboon* and USS *Carney* — conducted more than 95 intercepts of drones, anti-ship ballistic missiles and anti-ship cruise missiles and made more than 240 self-defence strikes on more than 50 Houthi targets. The USS *Dwight D Eisenhower* remained on station during March and April leading international naval forces protecting shipping in the Red Sea.

She sailed northwards and passed through the Suez Canal before arriving at the US Naval Base at Souda Bay on Crete on April 28, after 158 continuous days at sea. The USS *Dwight D Eisenhower* and her strike group fought an unprecedented battle against an opponent armed with advanced cruise missiles, strike drones and anti-ship ballistic missiles. This was the first time since the 1982 Falklands war, that a naval force had conducted extended operations under threat of enemy air and missile attacks.

ABOVE: F/A-18 Super Hornets form the 'Ike' started attack Houthi targets in Yemen on January 9, 2024. (US NAVY)

LEFT: US Navy E-2D Hawkeye airborne early warning aircraft played an essential role in monitoring threats to shipping in the Red Sea and passed 'real time' alerts of missile and drone launches to warships taking part in Operation Prosperity Guardian. (US NAVY)

BELOW: The 'Ike's' aviators kept up an unrelenting tempo of operations when the carrier was in the Red Sea as the US Navy came under intense attack by missile, drones and small vessels. (US NAVY)

Modern Carrier Tech

Putting Jets in the Air

What are the essential elements of an aircraft carrier? They are often nicknamed 'flat tops' and this implies the key part of an aircraft carrier is its long flat flight deck that allows aircraft to be launched and recovered.

Externally World War Two aircraft carriers look very similar to their modern-day successors. They have that vital flight deck, as well as an 'island' containing the ship's bridge and flight control centre. From here, senior officers control the ship and direct flight operations.

Around the flight deck there are large lifts to move aircraft up and down into the hangar underneath. This provides a sheltered space for engineers to carry out vital maintenance, protected from bad weather and sea spray.

These ingredients may look similar, but modern carriers incorporate very

different technology from their World War Two ancestors.

Modern carrier aircraft are far heavier than their predecessors. At 14 tons, a F/A-18 Super Hornet is twice the weight of a World War Two F4U Corsairs so needs help to get airborne.

In the 1950s, the introduction of the jet powered aircraft on carriers set off an exponential rise in the weight of carrier-based aircraft. This was followed closely by the development of the steam-powered catapult, which literally 'shot' jets off the bow of

aircraft carriers. This required huge steam generating plants to create the high-pressure steam that powered the catapult. Starting with the USS *Gerald R Ford*, the US Navy is moving from mechanical steam catapults to electrically powered catapults. These require less machinery and few personnel to operate them. Other navies are watching closely as the American experiment and are expected to move to adopt this technology.

As well as catapults, US aircraft carriers are fitted with arrestor wires to 'hook' aircraft landing back on deck. Aircraft are fitted with retractable 'hooks' that catch, or 'trap', the arrestor wire, bringing it to a halt in a few metres. Catapult and arrestor wire systems are not surprisingly known as 'cats and traps'. As a result, US naval aviators have long been nicknamed 'tail-hookers'.

For nations that can't afford big 100,000-ton aircraft carriers, there are other ways to help launch high performance jets. In the 1970s, the Royal Navy introduced the 'ski-jump' to help it launch its Hawker Siddeley Sea Harriers FRS1 jump jets off the bows of its Invincible-class aircraft carriers. This was essentially a ramp that gave the Sea Harrier extra-momentum to propel it into the air.

The Russian, Indians and Chinese have since adopted it on their aircraft carriers to help launch high performance jets without having to install catapults. Their carriers are fitted with arrestor wires to allow jets to land back on board, so they are known as short take-off but arrested recovery (STOBAR) aircraft carriers.

Italian and Spanish 'Harrier' carriers are fitted with ski jumps to allow them to operate vertical take-off and landing (VTOL) McDonnell Douglas AV-8B Harriers or Lockheed Martin F-35B Lightning II jump jets.

While the external appearance of modern aircraft carriers does not seem to have changed much over the decades, however, internally the vessels of the 21st century incorporate far more advanced technology.

The internal design of aircraft carriers is driven by the need to maximise the efficiency of loading weapons on aircraft and then turning aircraft around between sorties. At the same time experience in World War Two showed that aircraft, aviation fuel and bombs needed to be kept separate as much as possible to stop catastrophic explosions and fires. The devastation of Japanese aircraft carriers at the Battle of Midway showed the dangers of having bombs positioned too close to aircraft on flight decks or in hangars. As a result, magazines containing bombs and missiles were positioned below the waterline of aircraft carriers. This was intended to allow magazines to be quickly flooded if fire threatened to engulf them.

This, however, had serious implications for the movement of bombs and missiles up to the flight »

ABOVE: India and China have both put to sea their own locally designed and built aircraft carriers over the past two years. (DRAJAY1976)

BELOW: The 5th generation F-35 Lightning is the first carrier-borne combat aircraft to incorporate true stealth or low observable features. (MOD/CROWN COPYRIGHT)

RIGHT: Turkey is building a new fleet of combat drones to fly off its new aircraft carrier.
(TOLGAOZBEKCOM)

decks to be loaded on aircraft. It meant that weapons had to be manoeuvred through several decks and past watertight doors, taking a long time to bring bombs onto the flight deck. It was also very labour intensive, requiring hundreds of sailors to move trolleys loaded with bombs around the ship.

In the 21st century, the design of armaments handling systems have been transformed. The British Queen Elizabeth-class aircraft carriers are fitted with an automated system that is designed to allow weapons to be moved from magazines to the flight deck with limited human involvement. Weapons are moved via a series of automated lifts that bring them up to the hanger deck. Watertight and fireproof doors ensure that fire does not threaten the ship's magazine.

This technology allows the crew size of the Queen Elizabeth-class carriers to be reduced considerably. A US Nimitiz-class aircraft carrier is 100,000-tons and has a crew of 6,000 sailors and naval aviators. This is compared to HMS Queen Elizabeth that comes in at 65,000-tons – two thirds of its American counterpart – but only has a crew of 1,600 sailors and aviators, less than a third of the crew required on the US nuclear-powered carrier.

The next evolution of aircraft carrier design is under way with several navies looking to bring unmanned aerial vehicles or drones onto their flight decks. The biggest difference will be the installation of the necessary control centres and supporting communications antenna to allow crew on the carriers to direct drones on flight decks and during their missions. Currently every large drone needs a human operator to control it, so if dozens of drones are embarked then each carrier will need to have a suitable number of control consoles installed. If crew sizes can be reduced, then cabin space could be converted into control centres.

Drones are generally smaller and lighter than manned jet aircraft so future carriers could be reduced in size to make them smaller and hence cheaper. This might well prompt a surge in building if they cost less to build. The most recent American carrier, the USS *Gerald R Ford*, cost $12.8 billion to build which has led many even in the United States to wonder if they can afford to replace all the ten Nimitz-class carriers. Anything that reduces the cost of naval aviation helps head off critics.

BELOW: The US Navy's new generation of aircraft carriers, the Gerald R Ford-class incorporate electromagnetic catapults to replace their old steam-powered technology.
(US NAVY)

Fujian-Class

People's Republic of China

China's third aircraft carrier has just finished fitting out at the Jiangnan Shipyard in Shanghai and is currently undergoing sea trials

She will be the first Chinese carrier to incorporate a catapult launch system to allow high performance fast jets and fixed wing airborne early warning aircraft to operate from her deck. Three catapults can be seen in images of the ship.

Work reportedly began in 2015 but few details have been made public, resulting in the more accurate information about her capabilities coming from studying commercial satellite imagery of construction work on the ship. Block modules of the ship's hull started to be moved into a dry dock in May 2020, allowing the shape and size of the ship to be determined for the first time.

Senior People's Liberation Army Navy (PLAN) officers say the carrier is to have electro-magnetic catapults, rather than the old-style steam catapults that are currently used in US and French carriers. This will allow her to launch fast performance fighter jets and fixed early warning aircraft. The US Navy has introduced its own electro-magnetic catapult on its Gerald R Ford-class carriers, but the system has been beset by technical problems.

Her length, from bow to stern is more than 300 metres and she has flight deck that is more than 80 metres wide, suggesting she could end up similar in size and weight to the old US Navy Kitty Hawk-class carriers that came in at some 325 metres long and more than 80,000 tons. This would indicate that the PLANS *Fujian* could boast an air group of around 70 fixed wing aircraft when she puts to sea. Her crew are already moving onto the ship and imagery shows that mock-up aircraft have been moved aboard to practice deck handling drills. The ship put to sea to begin her sea trials on April 30, 2024.

FUJIAN CLASS	
Displacement:	79,000 tons
Length:	316 m (1,036 ft 9 in)
Beam:	39.5 m (129 ft 7 in)
Draught:	9.43 m (30.9 ft)
Propulsion:	Steam turbines, 8 boilers, 4 shafts
Speed:	30 knts (57 km/h) estimate
Complement:	3,000 estimate
Armament:	Type-730 CIW, HQ-10 point missile defense system
Aircraft Carried:	50-70 Aircraft or Helicopters

ABOVE: The PLANS *Fujian* is the People's Liberation Army Navy's first indigenously designed and built aircraft. It has three catapults installed to launch high performance fighter jets and specialist fixed wing support aircraft. (MAXAR TECHNOLOGIES)

LEFT: Construction of the PLANS *Fujian* began at the Jiangnan Shipyard near Shanghai in 2015. (RAYSONHO)

Charles de Gaulle-Class

France

RIGHT: France became the second operator of nuclear-powered aircraft carriers when the FS *Charles de Gaulle* sailed on her maiden cruise in May 2001. (US NAVY)

The FS *Charles de Gaulle* is the flagship of the French Navy, or *Marine Nationale*. She is currently the only nuclear-powered aircraft carrier outside the US Navy and is also the only non-American carrier to be equipped with steam catapult launch systems.

Her design follows a 'traditional cats and traps', layout with an angled flight deck so aircraft can land while others are launched from the bow catapult.

The carrier is named after the leader of the Free French Forces during World War Two, who later rose to be President of France between 1958 and 1969. The new ship was laid down in Brest in 1989.

At some 45,000-tons the FS *Charles de Gaulle* was the largest warship in service with a European navy until HMS *Queen Elizabeth* entered service with the Royal Navy in 2017. The cost of the ship when it was completed ran to €3.1bn.

Throughout the 1990s, progress on the FS *Charles de Gaulle* was slowed because of budget cuts, and it ended up not being commissioned until May 2001, more than five years behind schedule. A series of technical issues were also discovered during her sea trials.

First the flight deck was found to be too short to safely operate the E-2C Hawkeye airborne early warning

aircraft so it had to be extended. Her nuclear reactor has been refuelled twice during the ship's life - in 2007 and again during a major refit in 2017-18. The ship's ammunition magazines have been upgraded to accommodate the ASMP-A nuclear-armed missile and the SCALP EG air-launched cruise missile. Enhanced satellite communications systems have also been fitted to the ship.

The FS *Charles de Gaulle* sailed from her home port at Toulon, on France's Mediterranean coast for her first operational cruise on November 21, 2001, after she was ordered to join the US-led mission to defeat the Taliban in Afghanistan.

BELOW: The FS *Charles de Gaulle* follows a traditional design with an angled flight, deck, forward catapults and a single island. (US NAVY)

CHARLES DE GAULLE-CLASS

Displacement: 42,500 tonnes

Length: 261.5 m (858 ft)

Beam: 64.36 m (211.2 ft)

Draught: 9.43 m (30.9 ft)

Propulsion: Two Areva K15 pressurised nuclear water reactors (PWR), two Alstom steam turbines and two shafts

Speed: 27 knots (50 km/h)

Complement: Ship's company 1,350 and 600 air wing personnel

Armament: Four eight-cell A-43 Sylver launchers carrying the MBDA Aster 15 surface-to-air missile, two six-cell Sadral launchers carrying Mistral short range missiles and eight lat 20F2 20 mm cannons.

Aircraft Carried: 30—40 Aircraft Or Helicopters

Vikrant-Class

India

The Indian Navy is looking to expand its carrier aviation capability by building two new aircraft carriers over the next two decades. The first, the 45,000-ton INS *Vikrant*, also known as Indigenous Aircraft Carrier 1 (IAC-1), is capable of operating an air group of up to 40 aircraft.

She is the first ever aircraft carrier to be built in India and has been under construction at the Cochin shipyard in the southern state of Kerala since 2009. Indian companies have designed the ship and most of its major components. The ship started her sea trials in 2021 and Mikoyan MiG-29K landed on her for the first time in May 2023.

The 262 metres long and 62 metres wide ship is being built with a ski jump and arrestor wires to allow her to

VIKRANT-CLASS	
Displacement:	45,400 long tons
Length:	284 metres (932 ft)
Beam:	61 metres (200 ft)
Draught:	10.2 metres (33 ft)
Propulsion:	Eight turbo-pressurised boilers, 4 shafts
Speed:	+30 knots (56 km/h)
Complement:	110 officers and 1500 sailors
Armament:	4 × AK-630 CIWS, Barak 8 long range surface-air-missiles
Aircraft carried:	36 aircraft and helicopters

operate MiG-29Ks. Additional aircraft are being purchased for the ship and the Indian Navy are considering options including the French Rafale M and locally made HAL Tejas, as well as fixed wing airborne early warning aircraft such as the E-2 Hawkeye.

Following on behind the INS *Vikrant,* is the INS *Vishal* or Indigenous Aircraft Carrier 2 (IAC-2), which is proposed as being a 65,000-ton vessel equipped with a catapult launch system. The Indian Navy are looking to co-operate with foreign companies to draw on their experience of building super carriers, including

Britain's BAE Systems, France's Naval Group and Russia's Rosoboronexport. Negotiations have started with the US to supply electro-magnetic catapults for installation on the ship, which will also be built in the Cochin shipyard. This will allow far more capable fast jets, carrying bigger payloads and more fuel, to be operated.

The Indian Navy is also investigating operating unmanned aerial vehicles from the carrier, which is envisaged as entering service late in the 2020s or early 2030s. Once the INS *Vikrant* enters service the Indian Navy intends to retire the INS *Vikramaditya*.

ABOVE: INS *Vikrant* is India's first indigenously designed and built aircraft carrier. (INDIAN NAVY)

LEFT: The INS *Vikrant* is designed around the same short take off, barrier assisted recovery (STOBAR) concept used on the INS *Vikramaditya*. (INDIAN NAVY)

Vikramaditya-Class

India

RIGHT: INS *Vikramaditya* was converted from a former Soviet Kiev-class carrier and featured a ski-jump to allow MiG-29K fighter jets to operate from the ship. (INDIAN NAVY)

India's current operational carrier, the INS *Vikramaditya*, has a colourful history stretching back to the 1980s when she was commissioned into the Soviet navy as the Kiev-class cruiser *Baku*. With the demise of the Soviet Union, she became the *Admiral Gorshkov* but budget cuts in the resultant Russian Navy meant she was withdrawn from service in 1996.

In 2004 the Indian Navy bought the ship, and she began an extensive upgrade at the Sevmash shipyard in Severodvinsk in northern Russia. One of the key improvements was to install a 280-metre-long fight deck to allow her to operate Mikoyan MiG-29K/UBK supersonic jet fighters. The conversion stripped out the cruise and surface-to-air missile launchers from the forward deck of the ship and included the installation of arrestor hooks, as well as extensive modernisation of her machinery and electronic systems.

To boost the performance of the carrier's jets, a 14°-degree ski jump was installed on her bow. The ship can operate a mix of jets and helicopters, with a capacity to accommodate up to 34 airframes. As well as replacing its old Hawker Siddeley Sea Harrier FRS51s with Russian-made MiG-29Ks, the Indian navy ordered Kamov Ka-31 airborne early warning helicopters to replace its British-supplied Westland WS-61 Sea Kings.

The conversion of the ship was the subject of a long running dispute between the Indian Navy and the Russian shipyard with complaints of poor workmanship and sub-standard components being used. She broke down during her trials, which pushed back the handover date. There was also a dispute over the price of the conversion work and eventually the Indians ended up paying more than $2 billion for the ship compared to the initially agreed price of $1.3 billion. The delays meant INS *Viraat* had to be overhauled and extended in service.

VIKRANT-CLASS	
Displacement:	45,000 tons
Length:	262 m (860 ft)
Beam:	62 m (203 ft)
Draught:	8.4 m (28 ft)
Propulsion:	4 × General Electric LM2500 Gas Turbine
Speed:	30 kn (56 km/h)
Complement:	196 officers, 1,449 sailors
Armament:	2 × 32 cell VLS Barak 8 SAM, 4 × AK-630 CIWS
Aircraft Carried:	36 Aircraft or Helicopters

BELOW: The INS *Vikramaditya* (left) now serves alongside the INS *Vikrant* (right) to give the Indian Navy a two-carrier fleet for the first time. (INDIAN NAVY)

Giuseppe Garibaldi-Class

Italy

The ITS *Giuseppe Garibaldi* was laid down in 1981 as a helicopter equipped anti-submarine warfare ship. She is named after the 19th century hero of Italian re-unification and was the first ever 'flat top' to enter service with the *Marina Militare*.

The ship was commissioned in 1985 and for the first decade she operated Agusta AS-61 Sea King anti-submarine helicopters. Under a 1937 Italian law only the country's air force could operate fixed wing aircraft which stifled the *Marina Militare's* ambition to field Harrier jump jets.

Trials of Harriers took place on the Italian helicopter cruiser ITS *Andrea Doria* in the later 1960s, but it was not until 1989 that the Italian government changed the law and gave its navy approval to buy McDonnell Douglas AV-8Bs Harriers. The ITS *Giuseppe Garibaldi* can embark an air group of up to 18 AV-8B or helicopters.

In 2003, she underwent a major overhaul to install improved communications and extend the flight deck by removing air defence weapons from the rear deck.

GIUSEPPE GARIBALDI-CLASS

Displacement: 13,930 long tons

Length: 180.2 m (591 ft)

Beam: 33.4 m (110 ft)

Draught: 8.2 m (27 ft)

Propulsion: Four General Electric/Avio LM2500 gas turbines

Speed: 30kts (56km/h; 35mph)+

Complement: 830 crew, including 180 in air group and 100 command staff

Armament: Two Mk.29 octuple launchers for Sea Sparrow/Selenia Aspide surface-to-air missile, three Oto Melara Twin 40L70 DARDO guns and two 324mm triple torpedo tubes

Aircraft carried: Up to 18 fixed wing aircraft and helicopters

BELOW: The ITS *Giuseppe Garibaldi* was Italy's first operational aircraft carrier after it began embarking AV-8B Harrier jump jets in 1989. (US NAVY)

Cavour-Class

Italy

The Italian *Marina Militare's* second aircraft carrier is designed as a multi-role platform that can switch between air, amphibious, anti-submarine, and humanitarian operations.

ITS *Cavour* was laid down in 2001 at Fincantieri's shipyard in Riva Trigoso and was launched three years later. The ship was eventually commissioned into the *Marina Militare* in June 2009.

It was built with a 244-metre flight deck and 14° ski jump to allow the operation of McDonnell Douglas AV-8B Harrier jump jets. Her flight deck and hangar usually allow either 16 Harriers or Lockheed Martin F-35B Lightning II jumps jets or 12 helicopters, usually a mix of EH101s, NH 90s, or SH-3Ds, to be embarked. There are two 30-ton aircraft lifts up to the flight deck from the hangar and two 15-ton lifts for aircraft ordnance. When operating as an aircraft carrier the ship can accommodate 10 AV-8Bs or F-35Bs in the hangar deck and take five or six on deck.

The 27,000-ton carrier is designed with two roll-on, roll-off ramps to load vehicles onto docksides or landing craft. Up to 100 vehicles can be accommodated in the hangar deck and moved to the well deck by internal ramps. As well as her 486 strong crew, the ship usually accommodates 211 air wing staff, 140 task force command staff and 450 marines. The ship also has a large hospital with three operating theatres.

When the ITS *Cavour* first entered service, she usually embarked a fixed air component of AV-8Bs. Italy has since joined the F-35 programme and it now intends to take delivery of 15 B variants that can operate in vertical take-off and landing mode, using their revolutionary lift-fan system. The ship underwent a 16-month programme of modifications at the Military Maritime Arsenal in Taranto to allow her to operate the F-35B. The flight deck was reinforced with heat resistant coating to protect it from the hot exhaust of the jet's lift fan. Other modifications included improvements to the ship's hangar, equipment store, aviation fuel storage, data distribution network, sensors, and electronics.

CAVOUR-CLASS
Displacement: 26,700 long tons
Length: 244 m (800 ft 6 in)
Beam: 29.1 m (95 ft 6 in)
Draught: 8.7 m (28 ft 7 in)
Propulsion: Four General Electric/Avio LM2500+ gas turbines, two shafts
Speed: +29 knots (54 km/h; 33 mph)
Complement: 1,202 crew with option to surge additional 90
Armament: Four 8-cell A-43 Sylver launchers carrying the MBDA Aster 15 surface-to air missile, two Oto Melara 76/62 mm Strales guns, three Oerlikon Contraves 25/80 mm anti-aircraft guns
Aircraft carried: Up to 25 fixed wing aircraft or helicopters

Trieste-Class

Italy

Italy's newest 'flat top' vessel, the ITS *Trieste* is officially classified as a landing helicopter dock. She is the largest vessel in the *Marina Militare*.

The ship was ordered as part of the 2014–2015 naval programme and was built at the Castellammare di Stabia shipyards of Fincantieri. The first steel plate was cut on July 12, 2017, and the ship was launched and christened on May 25, 2019, in the presence of Italian President Sergio Mattarella, with his daughter serving as the ship's godmother. The first sea trial took place in August 2021, off the coast of La Spezia.

The innovative design is inspired by the style adopted by the British Queen Elizabeth-class aircraft carriers to maximise the efficiency of its flight operations. It features two distinct islands, the first is for navigation and contains the ship's bridge. The second is designated for the management and control of flight operations. This configuration provides greater visual range, more space on the flight deck, and a smoother and more efficient management of flight activities. The ship is equipped with a floodable well deck below the hangar to allow for the operation of landing craft to deliver marines to shore during amphibious landings.

Like ITS *Cavour* and ITS *Giuseppe Garibaldi*, the ITS *Trieste* also features a ski-jump on the flight deck to facilitate the takeoff of Lockheed Martin F-35B Lightning II jump jet.

The ship features a flight deck that has nine take-off spots for heavy helicopters or F-35B fighter jets. In full operational conditions, the ship can carry a total of 30–34 aircraft in various combinations of jets and helicopters.

ABOVE: The ITS *Trieste* features the two-island concept adopted on the British Queen Elizabeth-class carriers. (@WARSHIPCAM)

BELOW: The ITS *Trieste* is now complete and is undergoing sea trials ahead of entering service later this year. (IKI90)

TRIESTE-CLASS
Displacement: 37,000 long tons
Length: 245 m (803 ft 10 in)
Beam: 47 m (154 ft 2 in)
Draft: 7.2 m (23 ft 7 in)
Propulsion: CODOG + electric engines
Speed: 25 knots (46 km/h; 29 mph)
Complement: 460 crews, plus 604 embarked marines
Armament: 2 × 8-cell SYLVER A50 VLS for 16 Aster 15 and 30 missiles or 32 CAMM ER missiles
Aircraft carried: usually 12 × AgustaWestland AW101 or combination with SH90A, AW129D and F-35B

Izumo-Class

Japan

RIGHT: The JS *Kaga*to is currently being converted to allow her to operate F-35B Lightning II jump jets. (INDIAN NAVY)

IZUMO-CLASS	
Displacement: 27,000 tons	
Length: 813ft 8in (248m)	
Beam: 124ft 8in (38m)	
Draft: 24ft 7in (7.5m)	
Propulsion: Four GE/IHI LM2500IEC gas turbines	
Speed: 30kts (35mph; 56kph)	
Complement: 970 including crew and embarked troops	
Armament: Three Phalanx CIWS and two SeaRAM CIWS	
Aircraft carried: 28 aircraft or helicopters	

The 27,000-ton *JS Izumo* was commissioned into JMSDF service in 2015. She was then the largest Japanese warship to be built since the end of World War Two. The ship is named after the province and an Imperial Japanese Navy armoured cruiser also bore the name in 1898. Work began at the IHI Marine United shipyard in Yokohama in 2011, with the carrier projected as costing $1.5 billion. The *JS Izumo* and her sister ship were originally designated as a "multi-purpose operation destroyer" because the country's constitution prohibits the fielding of offensive weapons by the JMSDF that could project power beyond Japan's territorial waters.

Up to 28 aircraft or helicopters can be embarked on the ship, along with 400 marines and 50 3.5-ton small trucks, with helicopter spots on the deck to allow simultaneous operations by five helicopters.

In December 2018, the Japanese government decided that it would buy F-35B Lightning jump jets so they could be embarked on the Izumo-class ships. Plans were made to convert *JS Izumo* and JS *Kaga* to carry up to 14 F-35Bs and an order for 40 of the jets is in the process of being placed. Japanese Ground Self Defence Force V-22 Osprey tiltrotors are also expected to operate from the ship.

The conversion of both ships involved the strengthening of the flight deck by the application of heat-resistant coating to protect it from the hot exhaust from the F-35B's lift-fan system. A new power-supply system was also installed to enable F-35B operations and the ship's bow shape is also to be changed. The first stage of the conversion of *JS Izumo* is scheduled to be complete by 2024. A further modification is planned from late 2024 to alter the shape of the bow and the interior compartments to make aircraft operation and maintenance more efficient. There are currently no plans to install a ski jump. Work on JS *Kaga* is to follow on after the modification to the *JS Izumo*.

RIGHT: During 2024 the *JS Izumo* is to head to the East Coast of the US to carry out integration trials to allow her to operate F-35B Lightning II jump jets. (JAPANESE MOD)

Kuznetsov-Class

Russian Federation

Russia's only aircraft carrier is known universally as the RFS *Admiral Kuznetsov* and is named after the head of Soviet naval forces during World War Two.

The 43,000-ton ship has had a very long and chequered history since the Soviet military ordered her to be built in 1981. Work began at the Nikolayev shipyard on the Black Sea, which is now in independent Ukraine, in 1982. The ship sailed for her first sea trials in 1989 but was not fully complete.

In the dying days of the Soviet Union, she sailed from Nikolayev

KUZNETSOV-CLASS
Displacement: 57,700 long tons
Length: 305 m (1,001 ft)
Beam: 72 m (236 ft)
Draft: 10 m (33 ft0
Propulsion: Eight turbo-pressurised boilers and four fixed pitch propellers
Speed: 29 kts (33 mph; 54 km/h)
Complement: 1,690 ship's crew and 626 air group personnel
Armament: Six AK-630 300m anti-aircraft guns, eight CADS-N-1 Kashtan CIWS and 3K87 Kortik surface-to-air missile system, 12 P-700 Granit surface-to-surface missiles and 3K95 Kinzhal surface-to-air missile system, RBU-12000 UDAV-1 ASW rocket launchers
Aircraft carried: 30 aircraft and helicopters

and transited the Bosporus and Mediterranean before heading to her new home at Severomorsk to join the Northern Fleet. Her departure from the Nikolayev yard meant she escaped falling under the control of the newly independent Ukraine and suffering the fate of being sold off, as happened to her sister ship, the *Varyag*. This ship was eventually bought by China. The Chinese built another ship of the class using blueprints bought off the Ukrainians.

The ship's hull design is derived from the 1982 Kiev-class but is larger in both length and beam. The Kuznetsov-class is the first Soviet carrier to be designed with a full-length flight deck. The ship's 12 anti-ship cruise missiles are located in

launchers below the flight deck, just aft of the ski-jump.

The aircraft carriers are of a STOBAR (short take-off barrier arrested recovery) configuration. Short take-off is achieved by using a 12-degree ski-jump on the bow. There is also an angled deck with arresting wires, which allows aircraft to land without interfering with launching aircraft. The flight deck has a total area of 14,700 square metres. Two aircraft elevators, on the starboard side forward and aft of the island, move aircraft between the hangar deck and the flight deck.

The formal demise of the Soviet Union in December 1991 meant the RFS *Admiral Kuznetsov* by default became the flag ship of the newly established navy of the Russian Federation.

ABOVE: RFS *Admiral Kuznetsov* incorporate a ski jump to allow her to launch high performance fighter jets. (US NAVY)

BELOW: China bought the unfinished RFS *Varyag* and towed her to Far East where she was completed as the People's Liberation Army Navy's second carrier. (US NAVY WAR COLLEGE)

Queen Elizabeth-Class

United Kingdom

BOTTOM: HMS *Prince of Wales* **lead a NATO carrier battlegroup off the coast of Norway in February and March 2024 during Exercise Steadfast Defender.** (MOD/CROWN COPYRIGHT)

The first of the new Queen Elizabeth-class aircraft carriers is named after the World War One-era super dreadnought battleship, HMS *Queen Elizabeth*, which in turn was named after the Tudor monarch, Queen Elizabeth, who famously oversaw the defeat of the Spanish Armada in 1588. The modern HMS *Queen Elizabeth* carries the battle honours and crest – a Tudor rose - of the original battleship.

She is the largest ever Royal Navy warship and the most expensive surface ship yet built in the United Kingdom. After a decade of development and design work, the formal go-ahead for the two 65,000-ton Queen Elizabeth-class aircraft carriers was announced in July 2007.

BELOW: The Queen Elizabeth-class design features two islands and lifts to carry aircraft up and down from the flight deck. (MOD/CROWN COPYRIGHT)

QUEEN ELIZABETH-CLASS		
Displacement: 65,000 tons		
Length: 280 m (920 ft)		
Beam: 73 m (240 ft)		
Draught: 11 metres		
Speed: 25 kts (46 km/h)		
Capacity: 1,600, of which 679 are usually the ship's crew		
Armament: Three Phalanx CIWS, four 30mm DS30M Mk2 guns and six mini-guns		
Aircraft carried: 40 aircraft and helicopters (65+ aircraft surge capacity)		
Aircraft carried: 30 aircraft and helicopters		

The two ships were contracted to cost £3.9 billion. Work began on the construction of HMS *Queen Elizabeth* in July 2009 with the first steel being cut at BAE Systems' Govan shipyard in Glasgow. Her sister ship, HMS *Prince of Wales,* was built to the same design and was commissioned into the fleet in 2019.

The first phase of the project included the fabrication of 'ship blocks' at six shipyards around the UK, which incorporated key structural elements, as well as piping and electrical wiring. Each block was then floated on large barges to Babcock International's Rosyth dockyard in Fife, where the final assembly of the ship was being conducted under the umbrella of the Aircraft Carrier Alliance, which was led by BAE Systems and Babcock.

The first two blocks were welded together at Rosyth in June 2011 and over the next two years the ship took shape. She was 80% complete by September 2013 and was formally named by HMS *Queen Elizabeth* on July 4, 2014. Thirteen days later she was floated out of the Rosyth dry dock in the shipyard's basin to allow the final fitting out to begin.

This was largely complete by mid-2017 and on June 26 of that year she was manoeuvred out of the basin into the Firth of Forth to begin her contractors' sea trials. After a brief visit to Invergordon anchorage the

following month to inspect possible damage to her propeller shafts, she set sail for her new home at HM Naval Base Portsmouth and arrived on August 16. The ship was formally accepted by the Royal Navy on December 7 during a ceremony while she was docked at Portsmouth. The final costs of the two Queen Elizabeth–class carriers have now been confirmed by the Ministry of Defence to be £6.1 billion.

During February 2018, HMS *Queen Elizabeth* carried out operational sea training in the Western Approaches before heading out across the Atlantic on August 18 to begin deck landing trials with F-35B Lightning aircraft

off the east coast of the United States. The first landing and take-off by a US-owned but British-piloted F-35B took place on September 25 at the start of the trials process.

After a technology insertion period in early 2019, which saw the installation of her Phalanx close in weapon system and advanced communications systems, the ship sailed for the United States again in August to carry out the first embarkation of the UK-owned F-35Bs of the Royal Air Force's 617 Squadron. Exercise Westlant 2019 also saw the first carrier battlegroup

deployment by the Royal Navy in a decade since the retirement of the Invincible-class carriers.

During the first half of 2020, HMS *Queen Elizabeth* carried out two training cruises in UK home waters to allow more F-35B pilots of 617 Squadron and the operational conversion unit, 207 Squadron, to practice deck operations. In the May 2021, HMS *Queen Elizabeth* embarked a squadron of US Marine Corps F-35Bs as well as aircraft from 617 Squadron before setting sail to the Far East for the Carrier Strike Group 21 deployment. Both ships are now commissioned into the Royal Navy.

ABOVE: F-35B Lightning II jump jets take off from the carrier's bow ski jump and then return on board after engaging their vertical landing system. (MOD/CROWN COPYRIGHT)

BELOW: The stern view of HMS *Queen Elizabeth* shows the carrier's large flight deck that can accommodate dozens of aircraft and helicopters. (MOD/CROWN COPYRIGHT)

Juan Carlos I-Class

Spain

Spain's flagship was laid down in 2005 and it was completed five years later to allow the *Armada Española's* old aircraft carrier, the *SPS Principe de Asturias,* to be retired. The ship is named SPS *Juan Carlos I,* after the former king.

The SPS *Juan Carlos I* was initially known as a Strategic Projection Vessel because of its multi-role capabilities. Her crew of 900 can be complemented by another 1,200 marines or passengers.

She has a ski jump to improve the performance of the *Armada Española's* McDonnell Douglas AV-8B Matadors, as its Harriers are designated.

Her flight deck and hangar can accommodate up to 30 helicopters when she is configured for amphibious assault operations or a combination of 12 Matadors and 12 helicopters when operating as an aircraft carrier. The ship's well dock can accommodate four landing craft or a single hovercraft.

SPS *Juan Carlos I* was one of the first major warships to be fitted with diesel-electric propulsion to replace old propeller shafts and it also has a pair of azimuthal pods. These rotate and mean it does not need rudders to direct the ship.

Spain's Navantia shipyards have since sold the design of the vessel to both Australia and Turkey.

BELOW: Spain's AV-8B Harrier II jump jets now fly off the SPS *Juan Carlos I.* (US NAVY)

JUAN CARLOS I-CLASS
Displacement: 26,000 long tonnes
Length: 757.3ft (230.82m)
Beam: 105ft (32m)
Draught: 23ft (6.9m)
Propulsion: Two × Propulsion pods
Speed: 21kts (39kph; 24mph)
Compliment: 261 crew, 913 marines and 172 air wing personnel
Armament: Four 20mm guns, Vertical Launch Missile System
Aircraft carried: Up to 25 aircraft and helicopters

Gerald R Ford-Class

United States of America

The USS *Gerald R Ford* is the world's largest and most expensive warship. She is named for the president who served between 1974 and 1977. She is the first new class of aircraft carrier to be built in the US since the late 1960s when the first Nimitz-class ship was ordered. Construction of the carrier began in 2005 and, from the start, she was intended to incorporate many advanced new technologies with the intention of reducing her crew size by 25% compared to a

GERALD R FORD-CLASS

Displacement:	About 100,000 long tons
Length:	1,092 ft (333 m)
Beam:	134 ft (41 m) (waterline)
Height:	nearly 250 ft (76 m)
Propulsion:	Two A1B nuclear reactors, with four shafts
Speed:	In excess of 30 kts (56 km/h; 35 mph)
Complement:	4539 including air wing personnel
Armament:	Two RIM-162 ESSM launchers, Two RIM-116 RAM, three Phalanx CIWS, four M2 .50 Cal. (12.7 mm) machine guns
Aircraft carried:	75+ aircraft and helicopters
Aircraft carried:	90 fixed wing and helicopters

Nimitz-class vessel and hence reduce her long-term running costs. The original contracts for the ship had been worth $7.8 billion but by the time she entered service these had almost doubled because of problems trying to make her advanced technology work effectively.

The most revolutionary feature of the USS *Gerald R Ford* is the incorporation for the first time on an aircraft carrier of an electro-magnetic launch system, known as EMALS, to replace the old steam-powered catapult previously used to launch aircraft. The EMALS uses an electric motor to propel aircraft at great speed off the carrier. The old hydraulic arrestor wires to 'trap' aircraft landing on the carrier are replaced with a new advanced arrestor gear system that uses a water turbine.

Some 162 new electrically powered aircraft and cargo lifts are used in the USS *Gerald R Ford* to replace the old hydraulically powered ones. These new technologies remove the need for labour-intensive mechanical machinery so allow the ship's crew to be reduced significantly and allow more rapid aircraft turnaround.

The most obvious difference from the old Nimitz-class ships is the location of the island towards the rear of ship. This allows for a larger parking area for aircraft and helps reduce the ship's radar cross section.

All the new design features are meant to contribute to increasing the daily sortie rate to 160, with a surge capability to rise to 270 sorties a day. This compares to the Nimitz-class routine sortie rate of 120 a day with a surge rate of 240 sorties.

ABOVE: After many teething troubles, the USS *Gerald R Ford* is now fully ready for action and has carried out operational cruises in European waters. (US NAVY)

LEFT: The USS *Gerald R Ford* incorporates new technology that means she required more than 1,000 fewer sailors to crew her. (US NAVY)

The monster Nimitz-class came to define the term 'super carriers' after the US Navy brought the ships into service 1975. Since then, France, Britain, China and India have all brought their own aircraft carriers into service.
(US NAVY)

Nimitz-Class

United States of America

The USS *Nimitz* is named after the World War Two Pacific Fleet commander, Chester W Nimitz, who played a leading role in defeating the Imperial Japanese Navy. He was the overall US Navy commander during the critical Battle of Midway, which turned the tide against the Japanese in the Pacific theatre of operations.

Midway was the first naval battle fought between aircraft carrier fleets so it was fitting that the largest aircraft carriers ever built by the US Navy – or any other navy – should have been named after the famous admiral.

At just over 100,000-tons the USS *Nimitz* was the biggest warship in the US Navy when she entered service in May 1975, but subsequent ships of the class ended up being larger due to modifications to their design.

The designers of the Nimitz-class learnt many lessons from the construction of the US Navy's first nuclear-powered aircraft carrier, the USS *Enterprise*. The new ships had only two reactors, compared to eight on the USS *Enterprise*. This saved considerable amounts of space that allowed more aviation fuel and ordnance to be carried than previous carriers. It also reduced the number of personnel needed to keep the reactors operating safely and simplified refuelling.

Although the layout of the ship, with its angled flight deck and single island, owed much to the 1960s era carriers, the Nimitz-class boasted additional armour protection around

ABOVE: The USS Nimitz dwarfs Indian and Japanese flat tops during naval exercises in the Bay of Bengal in 2017. (US NAVY)

the hangars to prevent the spread of fire following enemy attack or accidents. As a result of experience during the Vietnam War, internal design of the ships was improved to enhance the efficiency of moving ordnance up to the flight deck and maintaining aircraft in the hangar deck.

The USS *Nimitz* entered service in May 1975, within weeks of the US evacuation from Saigon so was the first carrier of that era never to have seen service in the South East Asia conflict.

Nine more Nimitz class-carriers were built over the next 34 years with the final ship of the class, USS *George HW Bush,* being commissioned in 2009. The design of the ship evolved over the decades with two sub-classes entering service. The Theodore Roosevelt sub-class was built with a modular construction process and incorporated added protection to her main magazine. The last two ships of the class, featured a redesigned island and the last ship, incorporated new technology destined to be used the Gerald R Ford-class.

Over the life of the Nimitz-class, the air wings embarked have undergone major changes. In 1975, she embarked Grumman F-14 Tomcat fighters, Grumman A-6E Intruder strike bombers and Vought A-7 Corsairs II attack aircraft. During the 1980s, the McDonnell Donnell F/A-18 Hornet started to arrive. In the 21st century,

the Boeing F/A-18 Super Hornet and Lockheed Martin F-35C Lightning took their place on the ship.

The carrier's nuclear reactors were intended to go 20 years between refuellings and the ship has a projected service life of 50 years. It had been intended that the USS *Nimitz* would retire in 2022 when the USS *John F Kennedy* was supposed to be ready to join the fleet. However, construction delays and technical problems with the Gerald R Ford-class carriers have put these plans in question and the USS *Nimitz* has had to continue in service.

NIMITZ-CLASS

Displacement: 100,020 long tons

Length: 1,092 feet (332.8 m)

Beam: 252 ft (76.8 m)

Draft: 37 feet (11.3 m)

Propulsion: Two Westinghouse A4W nuclear reactors, four steam turbines and four shafts

Speed: 31.5 kts (58.3 km/h; 36.2 mph)

Complement: Ship's company of 3,532 and air wing of 2,480

Armament: Two Sea Sparrow, two RIM-116 Rolling Airframe Missile, two Phalanx CIWS, Four Mk 38 25mm auto-cannon turrets, 10 0.50 cal turret emplacements

Aircraft carried: 90 fixed wing and helicopters

BELOW: The air wings of Nimitz-class aircraft carriers provide them with impressive airpower to strike at land and naval targets. (US NAVY)

Wasp-Class

United States of America

WASP-CLASS	
Displacement: 40,500 long tons	
Length: 843ft (257m)	
Beam: 104ft (31.8m)	
Draft: 27ft (8.1m)	
Propulsion: Two boilers, two geared steam turbines, two shafts	
Speed: 22kts (41kph; 25mph)	
Complement: 1,070 crew, with 1,687 embarked marine contingent, as well as 184 surge capacity.	
Armament: Two RIM-116 Rolling Airframe Missile launchers, two RIM-7 Sea Sparrow missile launchers, three 20mm Phalanx CIWS systems (LHD 5–8 with two), four 25mm Mk38 chain guns	
Aircraft carried: 26 fixed wing aircraft or helicopters	

ABOVE: USS Wasp and her seven surviving Wasp-class assault ships have been the backbone of USS Navy amphibious flotillas since 1989. (US NAVY)

Work on the USS *Wasp* began in 1985 as part of a major expansion of the US Navy's amphibious capabilities in the final decade of the Cold War. She was finally commissioned in 1989, only a few months before the collapse of the Berlin Wall.

The design of the ship, with her large well deck for landing craft and two hangars to support aircraft operations, proved to be ideal for the conflicts and humanitarian crises that unfolded in the 1990s and 2000s. As a result, the US Navy maintained a drum beat of orders for eight Wasp-class vessels through to 2002 when the last ship, USS *Makin Island*, was ordered.

The USS *Wasp* sailed for her maiden operational deployment in 1991 with a marine expeditionary unit embarked. She played an important role in Operation Restore Hope in Somalia in 1993. Over the next decade she was a mainstay of US Atlantic Fleet deployments, including to the Mediterranean and Middle East. From 2004, the USS *Wasp* was very active supporting US combat operations in Iraq and Afghanistan.

In 2007, she carried out the first operational deployment of an MV-22B Osprey squadron. She had previously trialled the Osprey during the early stages of the programme in the 1990s. During 2011, she was modified to operate the F-35B and the USS *Wasp* then carried out the first sea trials with the new jump jet to prepare to bring the aircraft into service. Two years later the *Wasp* was the first US Navy warship to go to sea on an operational cruise with a detachment of F-35Bs embarked. All the Wasp-class ships remain in service, apart from the USS *Bonhomme Richard*, which was scrapped after being devastated by a dockyard fire in April 2021.

RIGHT: The iconic AV-8B Harrier II jump jet has a couple years left in USMC service as the F-35B Lightning II is brought into frontline service. (US NAVY)

America-Class

United States of America

The America-class of amphibious assault ships are eventually intended to replace the eight Wasp-class vessels. They each cost $2.4bn to build and incorporated many of the features trialled on the USS *Makin*, the last of the Wasp-class, including gas turbines and enhanced electrical systems. The first two ships of the America-class, known as Flight 0 vessels, are intended to use only airlift to deliver their marines to shore so do not have

LEFT: The America-class assault ships are optimised to operate the F-35B Lightning II jump jet. (US NAVY)

AMERICA-CLASS

Displacement: 44,971 long tons	
Length: 844ft (257m)	
Beam: 106ft (32m)	
Draft: 26ft (7.9m)	
Propulsion: Two gas turbines, two shafts	
Speed: Over 22kts (41kph; 25mph)	
Complement: 1,049 crew, plus 1,687 embarked Marines with a 184-surge capacity	
Armament: Two Rolling Airframe Missile launchers, two Evolved Sea Sparrow Missile launchers, two 20mm Phalanx CIWS, two x 25mm M242 Bushmaster machine gun system	
Aircraft carried: 32 fixed wing aircraft or helicopters	

a well deck to accommodate landing craft. This allows extra-space for fuel and other aviation support facilities. The well deck is being incorporated on the third vessel, USS *Bougainville*, and other ships of the class.

Potentially, America-class vessels can accommodate a full load of 20 F-35B Lightning jump jets but are normally intended to operate a marine expeditionary unit that combines Lockheed Martin F-35Bs or McDonnell Douglas AV-8B Harrier IIs, Boeing MV-22B Osprey tilt-rotors,

Sikorsky CH-35 Sea Stallion heavy lift helicopters, Bell UH-1Y Huey utility helicopters, and Bell AH-1Z Cobra helicopter gunships. The first of the ships was formally commissioned into the US Navy in 2014.

The second of class, USS *Tripoli,* is the third US Navy vessel to be named after the first land battle fought on foreign soil by the US Marines in 1805. The battle is memorialised in the US Marines' hymn with the line, "to the shores of Tripoli". Three more ships of the class are being built.

BELOW: More than a dozen F-35B can be operated from America-class amphibious assault ships turning them into 'Lightning carriers'. (US NAVY)

SUBSCRIBE TODAY!

Receive A Free Gift

Receive A Free Gift

Aviation News is renowned for providing the best coverage of every branch of aviation.

Combat Aircraft Journal is renowned for being America's best-selling military aviation magazine.

Chinese Carrier Fleets

Enter the Dragon

RIGHT: The PLANS *Liaoning* was China's first ever aircraft carrier when she entered service with the People's Liberation Army Navy in 2012.
(JAPANESE MOD)

China's rise as a military power over the past two decades has seen it build up its navy in a bid to supplant the United States as the dominant naval force in East Asia.

In the little more than 25 years, the People's Liberation Army Navy (PLAN) has put two fully equipped aircraft carriers to sea and has more flat tops under construction to join its fleet in the very near future. This is a remarkable transformation and few navies in the world have been able to field aircraft carriers at such speed.

The PLAN's two operational aircraft carriers now regularly put to sea during confrontations with US and allied naval forces around the disputed island state of Taiwan.

China formally got into the aircraft game in September 2012, when the PLAN commissioned the PLANS *Liaoning,* and the country joined the elite club of nations that possess aircraft carriers.

Two months later, the first launches and recoveries of the Shenyang J-15 Flying Shark aircraft occurred in November 2012, with additional testing and training in early July 2013. With this first landing, China became only the fifth country in the world to possess high performance conventional take-off and landing fighters aboard an aircraft carrier.

BELOW: The PLANS *Shandong* is the flag ship of the PLAN's Southern Theatre Fleet and is home ported at Yulin Naval Base on the island of Hainan.
(MAXAR TECHNOLOGIES)

It was several years before Chinese carriers were fully operational.

Unlike US carriers, PLANS *Liaoning* is not well equipped to conduct long-range power projection against land targets. It is better suited to fleet air defence missions, where it could extend a protective envelope over a fleet operating in blue water service. The PLANS *Liaoning* was very much a 'starter carrier', that enabled the PLAN to train its first groups of pilots and deck crews in areas critical to conducting carrier aviation. This carrier has since been joined by the PLANS *Shandong* and the PLAN now uses its carriers as the centres of multiple carrier and naval battle groups.

The PLAN is now the largest navy in the world with a battle force of over 370 platforms, including aircraft carriers, major surface combatants, submarines, ocean-going amphibious ships, mine warfare ships, and fleet auxiliaries.

The PLAN's overall battle force is expected to grow to 395 ships by 2025 and 435 ships by 2030. Its force structure consists of three fleets with subordinate submarine flotillas, surface ship flotillas, aviation brigades, and naval bases.

Chinese military strategy revolves around several operational theatres that are joint military organisations that combine air, land, naval, missile and special forces under a single commander. Three operational theatres have naval forces assigned and two currently have aircraft carrier battle groups operating with them. A third carrier is nearing completion, and this will potentially enable each of the coastal theatres to have its own naval strike force, led by a carrier.

The PLAN's next generation of carriers, the new Fuijan-class – the first of which it is currently undergoing sea trials – will have greater endurance and an electromagnetic catapult launch system making it capable of launching various types of specialized fixed-wing aircraft for missions such as airborne early warning and electronic warfare. It will have an air group of around 70 aircraft. This will increase the striking power of a potential PLAN carrier battle group when deployed to areas beyond China's immediate periphery. The PLANS *Fujian* was launched in June 2022 and is expected to be commissioned in 2024. In May ›>

ABOVE: PLANS *Liaoning* is flagship of the Northern Theatre Fleet and has regularly operated off the coast of Taiwan. (PEOPLE'S LIBERATION ARMY NAVY)

BELOW: The US Navy and its allies keep a close watch on Chinese aircraft carriers whenever they put to sea. (JAPANESE MOD)

ABOVE: Chinese-built J-15 fighters are the main carrier-borne jets on PLAN aircraft carriers. (JAPANESE MOD)

2024 satellite images emerged of small 'flat top' carrier, dubbed Type 04, under construction at a shipyard on the Yangtze River. She had a flight deck of around 90 metres, suggesting the vessel could be the first of a new class of drone carriers. The ship was in an advanced stage of construction, indicating she could start see trials in 2025. A flotilla of escort cruisers and destroyers, as well as logistic support ships and fleet replenishment oilers are also entering service to allow the PLAN's carriers to range far from their home bases.

The PLAN carrier battle groups are assigned respectively to the Northern and Southern Theatre Fleets. The PLANS *Liaoning* is home ported at Yuchi Naval Base in China's Shandong province, close to the Bohai and Yellow Seas, as part of the Northern Theatre Fleet, which reports to the Northern Theatre Command. Its mission is to operate in the Yellow Sea and out into the East China Sea.

The Eastern Theatre Fleet is responsible for the waters, close to Taiwan, but it currently does not have an aircraft carrier battle group permanently assigned. It is believed that the Eastern Theatre Command would take control of any aircraft carriers and other naval assets operating around Taiwan during any Chinese military operation against the island.

PLANS *Shandong* is home ported at Yulin Naval Base on the island of Hainan and it is the flag ship of the Southern Theatre Fleet. It is a core element of the Southern Theatre Command and has the responsibility for naval operations in the South China Sea. As a result, it is in the forefront of the ongoing confrontation with the US and its allies in the South China Sea region.

Although Beijing reaffirms that 'peaceful reunification' is its preferred course of action, the Chinese mainland government continues to signal its willingness to use military force against Taiwan. Many analysts consider this unlikely, thinking the Chinese will employ a range of options to coerce Taipei, including cyber and attacks, naval and air blockades, or kinetic campaigns designed to force Taiwan to capitulate to unification or compel Taiwan's leadership to the negotiation table on the Beijing's terms.

A key element in ensuring the success of any coercive campaign against Taiwan will be the use of Chinese naval forces to head off any attempt by the United States to intervene. To do this, Beijing could seek to deter potential US intervention in any Taiwan contingency campaign. Failing that, the PLAN would attempt to delay and defeat intervention in a limited war of short duration. The PLAN practiced elements of several military options during its August 2022 large-scale military exercise aimed at pressuring Taiwan, and again in April 2023.

BELOW: The PLANS *Liaoning* was re-built from a former Soviet Kuznetsov-class aircraft carrier but incorporated many Chinese developed technologies and features. (PEOPLE'S LIBERATION ARMY NAVY)

LEFT: The PLANS *Shandong* was built from scratch in a Chinese shipyard but was based on the design of the Soviet Kuznetsov-class vessels. (GG001213)

Any air and maritime blockade of Taiwan would see the PLAN's aircraft carrier battlegroups play an important role. The Chinese describe this as a Joint Blockade Campaign which would employ blockades of maritime and air traffic, including a cut-off of Taiwan's vital imports, to force Taiwan's capitulation. Large-scale missile strikes and possible seizures of Taiwan's offshore islands would accompany any Joint Blockade Campaign in an attempt to compel Taiwan's surrender, while at the same time, posturing air and naval forces to conduct weeks or months of blockade operations if necessary. Beijing likely would complement its air and maritime blockades with concurrent electronic warfare, network attacks, and information operations to further isolate Taiwan's authorities and populace and to control the international narrative of the conflict.

The next step up the escalatory ladder could be the use of precision missile and air strikes against key government and military targets, including air bases, radar sites, missiles, space assets, and communications facilities to degrade Taiwan's defences, neutralise its leadership, or undermine the public's resolve to resist.

The conclusion of any Chinese operation against Taiwan could be what is dubbed a Joint Island Landing Campaign, which envisions a complex operation comprising interlocking campaigns for electronic warfare, logistics, air, and naval support. The objectives would be to break through or circumvent Taiwan's shore defences, establish a beachhead, build up combat power along Taiwan's western coastline, and seize key targets or the entire island.

In 2022 and 2023, tension over Taiwan escalated and the PLAN deployed warships around the island for a series of exercises in a show of force to intimidate its government and population. These exercises were seen by several observers as being a rehearsal of Chinese war plans.

During May 2022, PLANS *Liaoning* and her battle group forayed out into the South China Sea to conduct intense flying drills close to Japan's southern island chain and its mainland. Over a ten-day period, the carrier launched more than 100 sorties, which prompted the Japanese Air Self Defence Force to scramble its own fighters in response. The carrier was mostly operating near the disputed Senkaku Islands, near Taiwan, on the edge of the South China Sea at the time.

During the April 2023 in the United Sharp Sword military exercises, the PLANS *Shandong* and her battle group deployed in the Philippine Sea, where it simulated air and sea strikes on neighbouring Taiwan from waters close to Okinawa, according to reports from the Japanese military. PLAN jet fighters and helicopters took off and landed on the carrier 120 times in 48 hours. Taiwan's defence ministry also released a map that showed four Shenyang J-15 fighters flying to the island's east, with the Chinese military later confirming fighters from the PLANS *Shandong*, loaded with live ammunition, had "carried out multiple waves of simulated strikes on important targets".

The PLANS *Shandong* and its escorts passed through the waters south east of Taiwan to start its first training voyage into the Western »

BELOW: Both the two first generation Chinese aircraft carriers incorporate ski jumps to launch their J-15 fighter jets. (PEOPLE'S LIBERATION ARMY NAVY)

RIGHT: The PLANS *Liaoning* can launch two J-25 in quick succession off her bow ski-jump. (PEOPLE'S LIBERATION ARMY NAVY)

Pacific, just as the American carrier, the USS *Nimitz*, and her battle groups was sailing about 400 nautical miles east of Taiwan. During ten days of flight operations up to April 16, the PLANS *Shandong* air group launched 330 sorties. Japan scrambled fighter jets in response to this activity before the Chinese carrier returned to her home port at the end of April.

In October 2023, the PLANS *Shandong* led a naval task force into the Philippine Sea close to Taiwan for 12 days. A total of 420 fighter launches and recovery and 150 helicopter take-off and landings were conducted from the carrier. The Chinese warships operated northeast to east of the Philippines, with the carrier battle group sailing midway between the Philippines and Guam. This was the carrier's third deployment into the Western Pacific.

BELOW: During August 2022, the PLAN established several live fire exercise zones around Taiwan to intimidate the island state's government and population. (REPUBLIC OF CHINA GOVERNMENT)

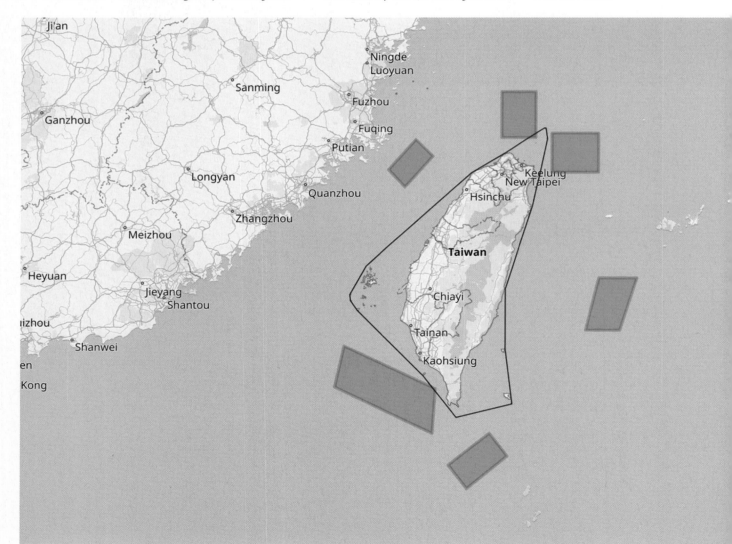

The foray by the Chinese aircraft carrier, prompted the US and Japan to deploy their own warships into the Philippine Sea, to the east of Taiwan. The USS Ronald Reagan and USS Carl Vinson, supported by vessels of the Japanese Maritime Self-Defense Force, and operated for several days in waters south of Okinawa.

This naval confrontation took a new twist in December 2023, a PLAN task group comprising of the carrier PLANS Liaoning, two missile cruisers, a frigate and destroyer, as well as a fast combat support ship, participated in joint exercises with the Russian warships in the East China Sea near Japan's Daito Islands group, which lies around 224 miles southeast of Okinawa.

Chinese carrier deployments into the waters close to Taiwan have now become routine and international observers report that PLAN sailors and naval aviators are conducting themselves in a professional and effective manner. If a shooting war should ever breakout in the region, China's aircraft carriers can be expected to give a good account for themselves in battle.

LEFT: The PLANS *Fujian* is the PLAN's first fully indigenously designed aircraft carrier, and it features three electro-magnetic catapults to launch high performance fighter jets and support aircraft. (PEOPLE'S LIBERATION ARMY NAVY, VIA WEIBO)

Naha

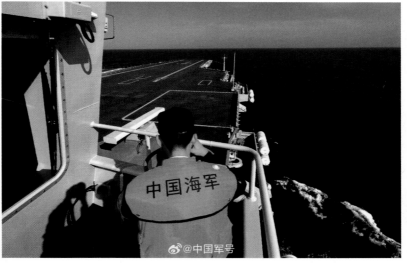

LEFT: After her sea trials in 2024, the PLANS *Fujian* is expected to start flying trials during early next year. (PEOPLE'S LIBERATION ARMY NAVY, VIA WEIBO)

BELOW: The PLANS *Fujian* during her first sea trials in April 2024, showing of her power and manoeuvrability. (PEOPLE'S LIBERATION ARMY NAVY, VIA WEIBO)

Beijing's Wings over the Sea

Chinese Naval Aviation

Chinese naval aviators belong to the air force of the People's Liberation Army Navy (PLAN) It currently fields a fleet of just over 700 aircraft and boasts 26,000 personnel.

The majority of its aircraft are land-based, which are a combination of air defence fighters, long range bombers and maritime patrol aircraft. Many of these aircraft still date from the time when the PLAN air force had responsibility for defence operations around China's coasts. Modern replacements are being delivered to improve the capabilities the PLAN's land-based aircraft.

In 2006, the PLAN launched the production of its first carrier-borne fighter jet, the Shenyang J-15 Flying Shark, which is the Chinese produced version of the Russian Sukhoi Su-33 (NATO: Flanker D). This is the navalised version of the Su-27, which features a strengthened under carriage, folding wings, a tailhook under a shortened tail stinger and a retractable in-flight refuelling probe on the left side of the nose.

The jet had canards, two-piece slotted flaps and larger wings for better performance during final approaches to deck landings. The Su-33 was designed to operate from the Kuznetsov-class carriers of the Soviet navy, which eventually made their way into Chinese service as the PLANS *Liaoning* and PLANS *Shandong*. The Chinese declined to buy the Su-33 from the Russians but opted to build their own version after obtaining blueprints for the aircraft from Ukraine.

The aircraft conducted its first take off from a simulated ski-jump on land on May 7, 2010, and the aircraft successfully performed its first takeoff and landing on PLANS *Liaoning*, China's first operational aircraft carrier, on November 25, 2012. The twin-seat variant, J-15S, made its maiden flight in November 2012 and a twin-seat electronic warfare variant, similar to the role of United States Navy's EA-18G Growler, dubbed J-15D, took its maiden flight in 2018.

In 2016, the J-15T prototype with catapult assisted take-off barrier arrested recovery (CATOBAR) capability began its test flight at PLA Navy land-based catapult facilities. These aircraft jets are intended to operate from the new catapult equipped PLANS *Fujian*, when it enters service. This aircraft has since evolved into a variant called J-15B, with new avionics, engines, and CATOBAR capability. It is intended to be capable of launching newer variants of the PL-10 and PL-15 missiles. The catapult-capable J-15 variant is in the final stage of the development and is currently testing from land-based steam and electromagnetic catapults.

More than 60 J-15s are now in service with another 50, believed to be the

BELOW: The J-15 is the Chinese built version of the Sukhoi Su-33 that operates from Russia's aircraft carrier. (PEOPLE'S LIBERATION ARMY NAVY)

ABOVE: The first successful landing of J-15 on a PLAN aircraft carrier took place in November 2012. (PEOPLE'S LIBERATION ARMY NAVY)

J-15T or B variants, on order. The jets are manufactured at Shenyang Aircraft Corporation's site in Liaoning province.

The PLAN's carrier-borne aircraft are based at airfields close to the main bases of the PLANS *Liaoning* and PLANS *Shandong*, in the Northern and Southern Theatre Fleet's areas, respectively. The home of PLAN carrier aviation is at Huangdicun airbase in the Northern Theatre Fleet zone. Shore-based training of carrier-pilots takes place at the base, which has a mock-up ski jump and flight deck layout on one of its taxi ways to allow pilots to practice landing on carriers.

There is an air brigade at the base, which provides the embarked air group for the PLANS *Liaoning*, which includes J-15 fighters, Z-9 and Z-18F helicopters. Another brigade

is forming at the base to be ready to operate from the PLANS *Fujian*.

The final operational air brigade is based at Lingshui air base on Hainan Island, close to the home port of the PLANS *Shandong*.

Once deployed onboard aircraft carriers, the J-15 jets operate mainly in the air defence role to protect Chinese naval tasks groups. They have short range PL-10 heat seeking and beyond visual range PL-15 air-to-air missiles. This later weapon is particularly important to keeping US aircraft and missiles away from Chinese warships.

The J-15 is a multi-role jet and can engage land targets and enemy ships with YJ-83K anti-ship missile, KD-88 standoff land attack missile and YJ-91 anti-radiation missile.

Airborne early warning is provided by a J variant of the Changhe Z-18

helicopter, which is fitted with a retractable radar. Another variant of the helicopter is fitted with a chin-mounted surface search radar, dipping sonar, and may be equipped with up to four lightweight torpedoes and 32 sonobuoys for anti-submarine operations.

The PLAN is also developing a carrier capable variant of the fifth-generation J-31 fighter, known as the J-35, which conducted its first flight in 2021. On October 29, 2021, the J-35 made its maiden flight. It is intended to operate from the forthcoming Type 003 aircraft carrier, PLANS *Fujian*, with an electromagnetic catapult system so has a catapult launch bar and a folding wing mechanism. If the J-15 is the equivalent of the US Navy Boeing F/A-18E/F Hornet multi-role jet, then the J-35 has been compared to the carrier capable Lockheed Martin F-35C Lightning II. »

BELOW: The Z18 can trace its heritage back to the French Super Frelon. It entered PLAN service in 2018. This is the maritime version, optimised for anti-submarine warfare. (PEOPLE'S LIBERATION ARMY NAVY)

PEOPLE'S LIBERATION ARMY – NAVAL AVIATION ORDER OF BATTLE, 8 APRIL 2024			
Unit	Aircraft	Role	Home Base
Northern Theater Fleet			
21st Naval Shipborne Helicopter Regiment	Z-9D	ASW/CSAR	Huangdicun Airbase
	Z-18J	AEW	
	Z-18F	ASW/CSAR	
HQ Carrier Air Wing for PLANS Liaoning			Huangdicun Airbase
10th Air Brigade	J-15/J-15S	Air Defence/ Strike	Huangdicun Airbase
11th Air Brigade (forming for PLANS Fujian)	J-15/J-15S	Air Defence/ Strike	Huangdicun Airbase
	Z-9Ds	CSAR	
	Z-18F	CSAR	
Southern Theater Fleet			
HQ Carrier Air Wing for PLANS Shandong			Lingshui Airbase
Air Brigade	J-15	Air Defence/ Strike	Lingshui Airbase
7th Naval Shipborne Helicopter Regiment	Z-8J	AEW	Sanya/ Yaxian Airbase
	Z-8F	ASW	
	Z-9C	ASW/CSAR	
	Z-9D	ASW/CSAR	
22nd Naval Shipborne Helicopter Regiment	Z-18F	ASW/CSAR	Sanya/ Yaxian Airbase
	Z-18J	AEW	

ABOVE RIGHT: PLAN naval aviators now have more than a decade of experience of operating fast jets from aircraft carriers. (PEOPLE'S LIBERATION ARMY NAVY)

RIGHT: The crews of Chinese aircraft carriers follow many traditions that are familiar to other navies, including doing mass sweeps for foreign objects that could be in-jested into the air intakes of aircraft and helicopters. (PEOPLE'S LIBERATION ARMY NAVY)

ABOVE: Flight tests are underway of the J-35 5th generation carrier-capable jet fighter after the aircraft made its maiden flight in 2021. (DAVID WANG)

Once in service, the J-35 will give PLAN carrier battle groups the ability to strike at heavily defended targets. Prototypes of the J-35 have been seen at flying from the manufacturer's plant but have yet to be seen operating from a ship. Once the PLANS Fujian completes her sea trials over the next two year, this will be possible.

Beyond fighter aircraft, the PLAN is refining the design of a carrier-borne airborne early warning aircraft, known as the KJ-600. A mock-up of the aircraft, which appears externally similar to the US Navy's E-2C Hawkeye, has existed for many years, and prototypes of the KJ-600 have been in flight testing since 2020. This aircraft is intended to operate from the PLANS *Fujian* when she enters service and mock ups of the aircraft have been seen in imagery of the carrier's deck.

Beijing is also developing the Harbin Z-20F helicopter for the PLAN, which is similar to the US Navy's SH-60 and will provide significant improvements in anti-submarine capabilities over the smaller Harbin Z-9 and Kamov Ka-28 helicopters the PLAN currently operates. It has yet to enter service in large numbers. The Z-20F will also complement the larger Z-18 medium helicopters that operate from the PLAN's aircraft carriers.

BELOW: The J-35 is being developed out of the FC-31 aircraft which is has been undergoing trials since 2012. (DANNY YU)

France's Strike Force

Europe's Nuclear-Powered Carrier

France has a long history of operating aircraft from ships, but the country's navy did not used carrier-borne aircraft in combat until 1947 when strikes were flown from the ex-US light carrier, the FS *Dixmude*, during the Indo-China war.

In the 1920s and 1930s, the French naval command was lukewarm about aircraft carriers and only one converted former battleship was ready for service as a flat top when World War Two broke out. The FS *Béarn* did not actually launch any aircraft into action during the war and ended up being used to carry cargo after she escaped ahead of the German occupation of metropolitan France in June 1940.

The French *Marine Nationale* had to rely on surplus British and US carriers, as well as second-hand aircraft during the 1940s and 1950s as the country tried to rebuild its armed forces and defence industry. During this period, the *Marine Nationale* acquired four surplus aircraft carriers to help it fight the war against Communist guerrilla armies in its Indo-China colonies. This experience established *Aéronavale* as one of France's elite air units. The exploits of *Aéronavale* pilots flying strike missions in Vought F-4AU1 Corsairs and Grumman F4F Wildcat during the battle to save the doomed French outpost at Dien Bien Phû in 1954 became legendary. Two years later, two French aircraft carriers joined the failed Anglo-French expedition to Suez in a bid to seize the strategic waterway from the Egyptians.

Its combat operations in the 1940s and 1950s, has shaped *Marine Nationale* carrier developments since, with it firmly believing that they should first and foremost be strike carriers. During the 1950s, work began on the first purposed designed aircraft carriers, the FS *Clemenceau* and FS *Foch*. For the time, these carriers were very modern and incorporated angled flight decks, arrestor wires and steam catapults. They were the first French aircraft carriers that could embark high performance jets, embarking Vought F-8 Crusader fighters and Dassault Étendard IV strike jets from 1961.

French defence strategy in the 1950s and early 1960s was still focused on securing its last imperial outpost in Africa but the withdrawal from Algeria led Paris to look at developing forces to work with NATO allies in the confrontation with the Soviet Union. The French government was keen to develop its own independent nuclear deterrent and the country's aircraft carriers have played an important role in this mission.

The *Aéronavale* has operated a fleet of nuclear-armed aircraft since 1962 with the Etendard IV on its Clemenceau-class aircraft carriers being armed with AN-52 nuclear gravity bombs. In 1978, the improved Dassault Super Étendard, entered service, giving the *Aeronavale* a stand-off nuclear strike ability with the Air-Sol Moyenne

Portée (ASMP) nuclear missiles. As the Clemenceau class retired from 1997 to 2000, the Super Étendard, remained in service on the successor, the FS *Charles-de-Gaulle*. Since 2010, the *Aéronavale*'s Dassault Rafale M F3 fighters embarked on the carrier have been armed with the upgraded ASMP-A nuclear missiles.

It had been planned to replace the Clemenceau-class with new nuclear-powered aircraft carriers in the late

1980s but funding problems delayed the project and work on the FS *Charles-de-Gaulle* did not begin until 1989 when her keel was laid. It took over a decade for her to be completed and finally enter service.

In November 2001, the carrier sailed from her home at Toulon naval base to join the international fleet in the Indian Ocean supporting the US-led campaign in Afghanistan hunting down the perpetrators of »

ABOVE: The FS *Charles-de-Gaulle* has a distinctive lay-out with its island position well forward, to allow aircraft to be parked along the starboard side of her flight deck. (US NAVY)

BELOW: US-made E-2C Hawkeye is the Aéronavale's carrier-borne airborne early warning aircraft. (US NAVY)

the 9/11 attacks on New York and Washington DC.

Super Étendard aircraft from the carrier carried out some 140 bombing and reconnaissance missions over the country. The carrier subsequently returned to the Indian Ocean and her aircraft again flew missions over Afghanistan in 2005 and 2010.

In 2011 the FS *Charles de Gaulle* played a leading role in the Libyan war, flying strike and reconnaissance missions as part of the NATO-led air campaign. There were few NATO air bases within striking range of Libya, so the carrier was able to bring her aircraft close to the country's coast and launch strike aircraft on missions that did not have to rely on air-to-air refuelling support.

Until she returned to port in August, the ship's aircraft flew some 1,350 missions over Libya. Two US Navy Grumman C-2A Greyhounds were assigned to FS *Charles de Gaulle* to conduct operational carrier on-board delivery (COD) missions during the intervention in Libya.

From 2015, the carrier was regularly deployed to the Eastern Mediterranean and Northern Arabian Gulf to launch aircraft to attack Islamic State forces in Iraq and Syria. Two cruises in 2015 were followed by deployments in 2016, 2019 and 2020. During these deployments, the French carrier was routinely integrated into coalition task groups, working with US, British and other allied navies.

Up until 2016, the FS *Charles de Gaulle* deployed with a mixed air group of Rafale M and Super Étendard combat aircraft, as well as E-2Cs and helicopters. After the retirement of the Super Étendard, the carrier deployed with Rafale fighters which by then had been cleared to fly in both air-to-air and air-to-ground roles. The Rafale M's ability to carry the Storm Shadow cruise missile, give the *Aéronavale* a deep strike capability and significantly enhances the strike power of the FS *Charles de Gaulle* carrier strike group.

In response to the Russian invasion of Ukraine in February 2022, the FS *Charles de Gaulle* moved into the Aegean and Ionian Seas to begin flying air

patrols over Romania and Bulgaria to reassure the NATO allies. The French carrier co-ordinated its operations with the USS *Harry S Truman*, which was also operating in the region.

In April 2024, the FS *Charles de Gaulle* Carrier Strike Group (CSG) sailed from Toulon for a six-week deployment in the Mediterranean, codenamed Mission 'Akila'. The French CSG is made up of the aircraft carrier, FS *Charles de Gaulle*, with its embarked air group comprising 18 Rafale M F3 aircraft, two Grumman E-2C Hawkeye tactical airborne early warning aircraft, and two Dauphin AS365 helicopters. A Forbin-class air-defence frigate, two Aquitaine-class frigates, a nuclear attack submarine and the new replenishment ship, FS *Jacques Chevalier* completes the CSG.

During the deployment, for the first time the French aircraft carrier will placed under the command of NATO's Naval Striking and Support Forces (STRIKFORNATO).

The French Navy is actively planning for a future aircraft carrier, which is expected to take over from the FS *Charles de Gaulle*, when she retires at the end of the 2030s. The carrier is known as the Porte-avions de nouvelle génération (PANG) or 'new generation aircraft carrier'. Construction of the PANG is expected to begin around 2031 and it is projected to enter service in about 2038. The ship will be nuclear-powered and will feature the Electromagnetic Aircraft Launch System and Advanced Arresting Gear.

FS CHARLES DE GAULLE AIR GROUP, MAY 2024			
Unit	**Aircraft**	**Role**	**Home Base**
4F	E-2C Hawkeye	Carrier Airborne Early Warning	Lann Bihoué
11F	Rafale M	Strike/Air Defence	Landivisiau
12F	Rafale M	Strike/Air Defence	Landivisiau
17F	Rafale M	Strike/Air Defence	Landivisiau
	AS365 Dauphin	Plane guard	Hyères
31FR	NH90 Caïman	SAR	Hyères
32F	H160M Guépard		Lanvéoc
33F	NH90 Caïman	ASW/SAR	Lanvéoc
34F	NH90 Caïman	ASW/SAR	Lanvéoc
35F	AS365 Dauphin	SAR	Hyères
36F	AS565 Panther	Small Ships Flight	Hyères

ABOVE: The Super Étendard was retired from the Aéronavale in 2016, passing the baton for fixed with carrier strike operations to the **Rafale M.** (US NAVY)

BELOW: US escort warships are often attached to the French carrier strike group to protect the FS *Charles-de-Gaulle.* (US NAVY)

Power Projection Force

Indian Aircraft Carriers

RIGHT: INS *Vikrant* and INS *Vikramaditya* are now in Indian Navy service, giving it a two-carrier capability for the first time. (INDIAN NAVY)

India considers itself to be a major political and military power in the Indian Ocean region and beyond. Since independence from Britain was secured in 1947, Indian naval power has grown as the country's economy expanded.

Today, India operates two aircraft carriers and has started a project to build a third carrier to allow continuous coverage when one of these ships needs to undergo essential maintenance. A new 75,000-ton nuclear-powered super carrier is being proposed as to replace the aging INS *Vikramaditya* and sustain Indian naval airpower into the second half of the century.

The Indian Navy has operated aircraft carriers for 63 years, and it continues to invest in naval aviation to protect its interests beyond the country's coasts. It has used it aircraft carriers for power projection missions in peacetime and during conflicts with its neighbour Pakistan, which were used in the strike carrier role to attack land targets.

BELOW: Indian Navy aircraft carriers routinely practice replenishment at sea tom demonstrate their ability to project power far from the country's territorial waters, across the Indian Ocean and beyond. (INDIAN NAVY)

Thanks to its close links with the Britain, the post-independence Indian Navy was strongly influenced by the Royal Navy's aircraft carrier experience. In 1957 it purchased the uncompleted 19,000-ton

HMS *Hercules* and paid for her to be finished at Harland & Wolff shipyard in Belfast. The Indians bought British Hawker Sea Hawk multi-role jets to operate from the ship, which was renamed the INS *Vikrant*, as well as Bréguet Br.1050 Alizé anti-submarine aircraft.

Within weeks over of being delivered in November 1961, the carrier and her air group was mobilised to support the Indian campaign to seize the former colony Portuguese colony of Goa.

INS *Vikrant* launched strike missions during the 1971 Indo-Pakistan war. Her Sea Hawks and Alizés pounded the enemy targets around Chittagong, Cox's Bazar, Khulna and Mongla, in the former East Pakistan, which is now Bangladesh. Heavy damage was inflicted on the ships and harbour installations. The runways at Pakistani airbases were rendered inoperable, and along with other units of the Indian fleet, INS *Vikrant*, ensured a total blockade off East Pakistan. The INS *Vikrant* helped to

prevent reinforcement of Pakistani forces from the sea, leading to the birth of Bangladesh.

In her day, the INS *Vikrant* was a very modern ship complete with steam catapult and angled fight deck, allowing her to operate Sea Hawk jets. In her final years in service, the carrier operated the Hawker Siddeley Sea Harrier FRS51 jump jet fighter. In 1986 she was replaced by the 28,000-ton INS *Viraat*, the former Royal Navy carrier HMS *Hermes,* and embarked Sea Harrier fighter jets until 2016 when the ship retired.

INS *Viraat* played a leading role in several high profile Indian military interventions, starting with Operation Jupiter in July 1989 to deliver a peacekeeping force to the island state Sri Lanka, off India's southern tip. She helped to deliver Indian army troops to Sri Lanka and then flying air support for them.

After gunmen attacked the Indian parliament in December 2021, the New Delhi government blamed Pakistani-based Kashmiri militants. A full-scale mobilisation of the Indian armed forces was ordered. Operation Parakram saw more than 800,000 Indian military personnel mass on the Pakistan border and INS *Viraat* was moved into position to lead a naval blockade against Pakistani ports. Diplomacy resolved the crisis, but it showed how the Indian intended to use their aircraft carrier to dominate the sea zone off its neighbour.

The Indian Navy got plenty of use out of INS *Viraat,* but in the

first decade of this century it was showing its age and work began to find a replacement. The India Navy wanted to set up their carrier capability by fielding a ship that could embark super-sonic fast jets. They turned to Moscow and ordered a former Soviet Navy vessel that could embark Mikoyan MiG-29k (NATO: Fulcrum) fighters using a short-take off, barrier arrested recovery, or STOBAR concept.

Russia's refurbished Kiev-class aircraft carrier RFS *Admiral Gorshkov* was commissioned into the Indian Navy as INS *Vikramaditya* at Severodvinsk, Russia on November 16, 2013. The 45,000-ton ship is over

285 meters long and 60 meters wide, making it the biggest ship in the Indian Navy at the time.

When the Indian Navy bought the ship, it was envisaged that she would remain in service for 40 years but the problems with poor work during her conversion led to speculation that she might have to be retired early.

Indian sailors and pilots travelled to Russia to be trained on the ship and their new aircraft before she sailed to India. A contingent of Russian technical support staff stayed on the ship for a year to make sure any breakdowns could be resolved. For a brief period, the Indian Navy had two carriers in service. Since entering service, the carrier ➤➤

ABOVE: India's first INS *Vikrant* entered service in 1961 and saw action in the strike carrier role during the 1971 Indo-Pakistan war. (ARUN PRKASH)

BELOW: The INS *Vikramaditya* entered service in 2013 after being converted into a strike carrier in Russia. (INDIAN NAVY)

INDIAN NAVAL AVIATION, MAY 2024				
Squadrons	Nick Names	Aircrafts	Role	Base
INAS 300	White Tigers	MiG-29K/ KUB	Air Defence/Strike	INS Hansa
INAS 303	Black Panthers	MIG 29K/ KUB	Air Defence/Strike	INS Hansa
INAS 321	Angels	Chetak/Allouette	Utility/SAR	INS Shikra
INAS 322	Guardians	Dhruv Mk 3	Utility/Surveillance/ASW/SAR	INS Garuda (Kochi)
INAS 323	Harriers	Dhruv Mk 3	Utility/Surveillance/ASW/SAR	INS Garuda (Kochi)
INAS 324	Kestrels	Dhruv Mk 3	Utility/Surveillance/ASW/SAR	INS Dega
INAS 325	Eagle Owl	Dhruv Mk 3	Utility/Surveillance/ASW/SAR	Port Blair
INAS 330	Harpoons	Sea King Mk 42B	ASW/Utility/SAR	INS Shikra
INAS 333	Eagles	Kamov Ka-28	ASW/Utility/SAR	INS Dega
INAS 334	Sea Hawks	HH-60R	ASW/Utility/SAR	INS Garuda (Kochi)
INAS 336	Flaming Arrows	Sea King Mk 42	ASW/Utility/SAR	INS Garuda (Kochi)
INAS 339	Falcons	Kamov Ka-31	AEW	INS Garuda (Kochi)
INAS 350	Harpoons	UH-3H Sea King	ASW/Utility/SAR	INS Dega
Marine Commando Flight	Zappers	Sea King Mk 42	Air Assault	INS Shikra

Notes
INS: Indian Naval Station
INAS: Indian Naval Air Squadron

RIGHT: The INS *Vikramaditya*'s Soviet heritage is clear, and she has much in common with the Russian Navy's Kusnetzov-class carriers, even though the India ship is based on the hull of a Kiev-class vessel. (INDIAN NAVY)

BELOW: The new INS *Vikrant* uses the same short take off barrier assisted recovery (STOBAR) concept as the INS *Vikramaditya*, but it incorporates Indian technology and equipment. (INDIAN NAVY)

has participated in exercises around the Indian Ocean region and in trials for the naval variant of the HAL Tejas Light Combat Aircraft, which was the first Indian-made aircraft ever to land on an aircraft carrier.

As well as the MiG-29K fighters, the ship embarked Kamov Ka-31 (NATO: Helix) airborne early warning, anti-submarine Kamov Ka-28 (NATO: Helix), multi-role Westland WS-61 Sea King and HAL Chetaks and HAL Dhruv utility helicopters.

LEFT: Indian Prime Minister, Narendra Modi commissions the first indigenous aircraft carrier as INS *Vikrant*, at Kochi shipyard in Kerela on September 2, 2022, which illustrated the importance of the ship to the country's defence strategy. (INDIAN PRIME MINISTER PRESS OFFICE)

The ship is home ported at Indian Naval Station Kadamba, Karwar, on India's south western coast, as part of the Western Naval Command, leaving her well positioned to intervene in any conflict with Pakistan.

India's carrier capability received another boost in September 2022, when the second INS *Vikrant* was commissioned into the Indian Navy. She is the first aircraft carrier to be designed and built in India. The 45,000-ton vessel currently operates MiG-29Ks as its main fast jet, but a competition is under way to buy either French-made Dassault Rafale-M or US-made Boeing F/A-18E/F Super Hornet multi-role strike jets to enter service early in the 2030s. The ship is currently carrying out flight integration trials ahead of being formally declared fully operational.

The carrier is home ported at Vishakapatnam as part of the Eastern Naval Command and this is an indication that the Indian Navy was wider ambitions for the INS *Vikrant*. The Indian government is moving closer to the United States out of mutual concern over growing Chinese influence in the Indian Ocean. It was buying advanced military equipment from the US, including Boeing C-17 Globemaster strategic airlifters, Boeing P-8A Poseidon maritime patrol aircraft and Sikorsky MH-60R Seahawk maritime helicopters. The Indian navy is building bases on remote island chains in the Indian Ocean and envisaging using her aircraft carriers to defend the bases against Chinese attacks.

India is also keen to use its maritime power to protect trade routes into the Arabian Gulf, Red Sea and Straits of Malacca. It has sent naval task forces to all these regions to secure freedom of navigation for Indian merchant vessels over the past two decades. Indian naval chiefs see its aircraft carriers as a means to boost the effectiveness of these interventions and ensure India's concerns are taken into account during international efforts to ensure freedom of navigation.

India's age-old rivalry with Pakistan is always present in New Delhi's defence planning and its growing carrier force ensuring that in the event of conflict with its western neighbour Indian naval forces will be rapidly able to defeat Pakistani naval forces and impose a tight blockade of its coast.

BELOW: Russian supplied MiG-29Ks are the Indian Navy's primary carrier borne fast jet after the retirement of the Sea Harrier FRS51 in 2016. (INDIAN NAVY)

Naval Airpower Over the Med

Italy's Aircraft Carriers

ABOVE: A new era is opening with the arrival of F-35B Lightning II 5th generation jump jet on the ITS *Cavour*. (US NAVY)

Italy pioneered the development of military air power before World War One and in 1911, the then *Servizio Aeronautico*, carried out the first use of heavier-than-air aircraft in armed conflict in Libya during the Italo-Turkish War.

Italy's admirals were less interested in operating aircraft from ships because it was thought the country's position in the centre of the Mediterranean meant it could provide air cover for its fleet from shore bases. As other countries pushed ahead with experiments with aircraft carriers, Italy's pilots were stuck flying from airfields.

This changed in November 1940, when the British carrier HMS *Illustrious* delivered a devastating and unforeseen attack on the main Italian naval facility at Taranto, crippling several important Italian warships. A few months later, the Italian fleet suffered more heavy losses to the British Mediterranean Fleet at

RIGHT: Trials of the F-35B began on the ITS *Cavour* in 2021 and the *Marina Militare* is in the process of growing its force of the jets to allow an operational cruise to take place. (US NAVY)

Cape Matapan, with aircraft from HMS *Formidable* sinking four Italian cruisers and two destroyers. Three British sailors were killed in the one-sided action. As a result, two cruise liners were ordered to be converted

into aircraft carriers in the response, but they were not completed before Italy was knocked out of the war in 1943.

As a result, Italy did not have a fully functional aircraft carrier until ITS *Guiseppe Garibaldi* was commissioned in 1985. Throughout the Cold War the *Marina Militare's* task was the surveillance of the Mediterranean region to help the US Navy prevent a Soviet breakout from the Black Sea. By the early 1960s the *Marina Militare* was going through a reforming period. Its strategic tasks were to control the chokepoints of the Mediterranean with naval and air power. The ITS *Guiseppe Garibaldi* was ordered in 1981 to fulfil Italy's strategic naval operations and finally acquired fixed wing McDonnell Douglas AV-8B Harrier IIs in 1989, after the country's laws were changed to allow the navy to operate fixed wing aircraft.

Italy's strategic situation in the Cold War revolved around dominating naval chokepoints with anti-submarine warfare helicopters and frigates, to prevent enemy submarines threatening vital naval assets or civilian merchant vessels. »

ITALIAN NAVAL AVIATION (AVIAZIONE PER LA MARINA MILITARE), MAY 2024			
Unit	Aircraft	Role	Home Base
1 Grupelicot	EH-101	ASW	La Spezia-Luni
2 Grupelicot	AB212ASW	ASW	Catania-Fontanarossa
3 Grupelicot	EH-101	ASW	Catania-Fontanarossa
4 Grupelicot	MH-90A, SH-90A, AB212ASW	ASW/Assault	Taranto-Grottaglie
Reparto Eliassalto	AB212ASW	ASW	Taranto-Grottaglie
Reparto Operazione Anifibia	AB2021	ASW	Taranto-Grottaglie
5 Grupelicot	MH-90A, SH-90	Assault	La Spezia-Luni
Gruppo Aerei Imbarcati	AV-8B, TAV-8B (transitioning to F-35B)	Air Defence/Strike	Taranto-Grottaglie
Centro Sperimentale Aeromarittimo	MH-101, SH-90	ASW	La Spezia-Luni

ABOVE: The first F-35B landed on the ITS *Cavour* on March 3, 2021, during trials off East of the Coast of the United States. (US NAVY)

BELOW: The ITS *Guiseppe Garibaldi* took part in NATO's Exercise Steadfast Defender off the coast of north Norway in the anti-submarine role, in the carrier's swansong before its expected retirement late in 2024. (MOD/CROWN COPYRIGHT)

ABOVE: Italian navy officers watched the first landing of a F-35B on the ITS *Cavour* with satisfaction, knowing that it secured the future of their carriers for the several decades. (US NAVY)

BELOW: Italy first acquired the ITS *Giuseppe Garibaldi* as an anti-submarine carrier to dominate choke points in the Mediterranean region. (MOD/CROWN COPYRIGHT)

Flat top carriers were considered very effective in this type of scenario because they could carry a large number of helicopters.

The ITS *Giuseppe Garibaldi* can carry up to 18 helicopters compared to destroyers and frigates which might be able to carry just one or two. Helicopters are the most effective weapon against submarines because of their speed and range. By using dipping sonar and torpedoes, helicopters can strike submarines directly without being attacked themselves. The Italian Navy acquired Harriers to use as fleet defence aircraft to protect its warships at sea from air attack, with actual strike operations against land targets as a secondary priority.

In addition, the large size of an aircraft carrier allows them to be used in humanitarian operations, flying the flag and diplomatic visits, and as a show and sign of a country's strength and prestige.

With the ending of the Cold War, the *Marina Militare* had to reassess its operational concepts and it soon found its aircraft carriers were even more useful in what soon became known as the 'New World Disorder'. The ITS *Giuseppe Garibaldi* found itself being used in a variety of roles, including as a strike carrier to attack land targets in support of Italian and allied peacekeeping troops.

In 1995, the ITS *Giuseppe Garibaldi* sailed to Somalia for her first combat cruise to provide air support for UN peacekeeping troops as they withdrew from the country. Her Harriers flew over 100 missions but did not drop any bombs in anger. It was not until 1999 that the ship's AV-8Bs got their combat debut during the Kosovo war, flying in support of the NATO air campaign. This was the first combat employment of carrier aviation by the *Marina Militare*. Between May and June 1999, the ship's Harriers flew 30 combat sorties, dropping laser guided bombs and firing Maverick air-to-ground missiles. In 2001, the ITS *Giuseppe Garibaldi* sailed to the Indian Ocean to support the US campaign in Afghanistan and her jets flew patrols over the land-locked nation. Some 160 laser guided bombs were dropped by the ship's Harriers during the 2011 Libya campaign.

The ITS *Giuseppe Garibaldi* found itself so much in demand that an extra carrier, the ITS *Cavour*, was ordered in 2001 and she joined the fleet in 2009. The ship was mobilised in early 2010 to lead Italy's contribution to Operation White Crane to deliver humanitarian aid to Haiti after an earthquake devastated the country. In 2013, she sailed to the Indian Ocean to work in the strike carrier role alongside the US and French aircraft carriers operating in the region.

In response to an increase in migrant flows across the Mediterranean from Libya in 2015, the European Union launched Operation Sophia to intercept hundreds of small boats carrying the migrants. The ITS *Cavour* was dispatched to the Gulf of Sitre to act as the flagship of the operation.

Italy was one of the first international partners to join the

project to build the Lockheed Martin F-35 Lightning II joint strike fighter. The *Marina Militare* ordered 15 F-35B jump jet variants to operate from its aircraft carriers, with the first aircraft being delivered in 2018. The ITS *Cavour* sailed across the Atlantic in the spring of 2021 to carry out ship-aircraft integration trials with aircraft of the US F-35 Integrated Test Task Force. These trails were successful and proved that the ship could safety embark and operate the F-35B. It is planned that initial operating capability (IOC) will be declared later in 2024 to make the full transition of the *Marina Militare* from the AV-8B to the F-35B.

The activation of the ITS *Cavour* as a 'Lightning Carrier' will allow the retirement of the veteran AV-8B. The ITS *Cavour* is home ported at Taranto with the 2nd Naval Division in the strike carrier role.

It is also expected that once the new amphibious assault ship, ITS *Trieste*, is fully operational the long serving ITS *Guiseppe Garibaldi* will be able to be retired. In her final months in service, the ITS *Guiseppe Garibaldi* took part in NATO's Exercise Steadfast Defender off the coast of north Norway in the anti-submarine role with AgustaWestland SH-101A Merlin helicopters embarked. This helicopter is one of NATO's most

effective ASW helicopters and give the *Marina Militare* a unique capability among Mediterranean navies.

Although it is planned that the ITS *Trieste*, will be based at Brindisi with the 4th Naval Division, which contains all the amphibious ships of the National Sea Projection Capability and the marines of the San Marco Brigade. This is Italy's main amphibious force, and it is held at high readiness to sail on rapid reaction missions, including humanitarian, peacekeeping and other intervention operations. The ITS *Trieste* will also be able to embark F-35Bs and act as a strike carrier when ITS *Cavour* needs to undergo essential maintenance.

ABOVE: Night take-off trials from the ITS *Cavour* in 2021 proved the carrier's ability to carry out strike operations around the clock. (US NAVY)

BELOW: The ITS Giuseppe Garibaldi was Italy's first aircraft carrier and is soon to retire. (US NAVY)

Far East Flat Tops

Japan's Carrier Rebirth

RIGHT: A US Marine Corps F-35B Lightning II lands on the *JS Izumo* in March 2021 to demonstrate that the Japanese ship can embark the jet. (US NAVY)

Japan has a long tradition of building aircraft carriers, stretching back to the 1920s when the Imperial Japanese Navy saw the potential of carrier-borne aviation as a war winning weapon to overturn US naval dominance in the Pacific. The surprise attack on the US Pacific fleet at Pearl Harbor in December 1941 confirmed the Japan as the leading exponent of aircraft carrier operations at the time.

Japan's defeat in 1945 and subsequent US occupation led to the country being disarmed. When the US allowed Japan to begin rebuilding its armed forces in the 1950s, the country disavowed the ownership of offensive weapons, which was taken to include aircraft carriers and amphibious forces.

Over the past 25 years, the modern Japanese Maritime Self Defence Force (JMSDF) has been steadily building up its naval capability, as tension has grown with China. Tokyo is looking to bolster the defences of the remote island chain that stretches down to within 108 kilometres of Taiwan. These islands mark the boundary between the East China Sea and the Philippines Sea. Some small uninhabited islands in this island chain have been claimed by China.

BELOW: The JS *Kaga* is the second ship of the Izumo-class, and she entered service in 2017, originally in the amphibious assault role with helicopters embarked. (HUNINI)

Work has been undertaken to convert the JS *Kaga* to be able to operate the F-35B, includes changes to the bow to make it square shaped. Further modifications will take place in 2026 to alter her interior to better accommodate the jets. (JMSDF)

As these islands are Japanese territory, operations to protect them are considered 'defensive' so the JMSDF was able to develop forces and capabilities to allow these islands to be reinforced, or if necessary, recapture them if they fall to the Chinese. The JMSDF first started building up its amphibious forces to allow ground troops to be moved to the islands or to land marines to retake them.

In the past decade, the continuing Chinese naval build up has prompted the Japanese to look again at how its forces could operate in its island chain. The JMSDF concluded that its amphibious forces needed their own air support and in 2018 announced plans to field its first aircraft carriers since World War Two.

Work has started to convert the amphibious landing ship *JS Izumo* and its sister ship, JS *Kaga*, into what the JMSDF terms as 'light aircraft carriers', or 'Lightning carriers', to allow them to lead a combined air-land task force.

In December 2018, the Japanese government announced that it would buy 40 Lockheed Martin F-35B Lightning jump jets so they could be embarked on the Izumo-class ships. Plans were made to convert *JS Izumo* and JS *Kaga* to each carry up to 14 F-35Bs.

The first of these aircraft are due to arrive in Japan during 2024 and they will be based Nyutabaru Air Base under the command of the Japanese Air Self Defence Force's 5th Air Wing. Although the F-35B would operate from the JMSDF ships in the future, the airframes and personnel are under the JASDF command. A dedicated training site is to be set up on island of Mageshima, including a mock-up of an Izumo-class ship's flight deck to allow F-35B pilots to practice take-offs and landings.

Later in 2024, one of the Izumo-class ships is to head to the Eastern seaboard of the United States to carry out integration trials with Lightning aircraft of the US F-35 Integrated Test Force. This is the same process followed by British and Italian aircraft carriers to allow them to safely operate the F-35B. Once full safety clearances have been established the JASDF aircraft will be able to take its aircraft to sea and re-establish Japan's aircraft carrier capability.

ABOVE LEFT: Japanese flat tops – JS *Ise* (rear) and JS *Izumo* (front) - exercises with the British carrier HMS *Queen Elizabeth*, during the vessel's deployment to the Far East in 2021. (MOD/CROWN COPYRIGHT)

Carrier Battle Force

Russia's Northern Fleet

ABOVE: Su-33 fighters provide air defence for Russia's carrier battle group and can strike at land and naval targets.
(RUSSIAN MINISTRY OF DEFENCE)

Russia has its own distinct way of employing aircraft carriers that owes a lot to the experience of the Soviet Navy during the Cold War.

The famous 'father' of the Soviet blue water navy, Admiral Sergey Gorshkov was determined to build up the Soviet fleet to rival the US Navy, but he was not about to simply copy every aspect of American naval power. The central element of Soviet naval power was its fleet of nuclear ballistic missile firing submarines or SSBNs. They were to be the invulnerable element of Moscow's nuclear deterrent and Gorshkov was determined to build a protective shield around them to stop US and NATO submarines and warships hunting them down.

Gorshkov envisaged creating what were dubbed 'submarine bastions', where the Soviet SSBNs would be safe from attack. The Soviet surface fleet was expanded to create the outer walls of these bastions, establishing barriers of anti-submarine helicopters to hunt down NATO attack submarines and carrier launched fighter jets would shoot down any NATO maritime patrol aircraft that ventured nearby.

The main Soviet submarine bastion was to be in the Barents Sea off the

RIGHT: Whenever the RFS *Admiral Kuznetsov* puts to sea allied naval force keep her under close observation.
(MOD/CROWN COPYRIGHT)

ABOVE: The RFS *Admiral Kuznetsov* flight deck and ski jump are at the heart of its ability to launch and recover high performance fast jets. (MOD/CROWN COPYRIGHT)

LEFT: Two Su-33 can be launched in quick succession over the RFS *Admiral Kuznetsov* ski jump. (US NAVY)

coast of the Kola Peninsula in the Arctic circle. A smaller bastion was to be established in Soviet Far East.

The Soviet Union was slow getting into the aircraft carrier business and it first developed Moskva-class cruisers embarking up to 18 anti-submarine helicopters. During the 1970s, it began to embark Yakolov Yak-38 (NATO: Forger) jump jets on a first generation of Kiev-class flat tops. In the 1980s, plans were laid to build a new fleet of short take off barrier assisted recovery (STOBAR) carriers. Work to develop a carrier version of the Sukhoi Su-27 (NATO: Flanker) supersonic fighter jet began in the late 1980s. This was known as the Su-33, and it was intended to take on and defeat, US Navy fighter jets that tried to challenge Russian warships protecting submarine bastions.

All these plans turned to dust in the chaotic collapse of the Soviet Union in the early 1990s and only one of the Kuznetsov-class carriers was left in service. The newly formed Russian Navy managed to get her out of port in Ukraine before the country declared itself independent in 1992. The second carrier was not completed and was eventually sold by the Ukrainians to China.

The navy of the new Russian Federation adopted the Soviet Navy's bastion strategy and the RFS *Admiral Kuznetsov* and her supporting battle group continued to focus on dominating the waters of the ➤➤

ABOVE: A squadron of Ka-28 anti-submarine helicopter is usually embarked on the RFS *Admiral Kuznetsov* to help it establish a 'bastion' to protect Russian nuclear deterrent submarines.
(RUSSIAN MINISTRY OF DEFENCE)

RIGHT: The RFS *Admiral Kuznetsov* is the pride of the Northern Fleet, and it is used on flag waving visits to foreign ports to demonstrate Russian military might.
(RUSSIAN MINISTRY OF DEFENCE)

Barent Sea, in co-operation with land-based air power, anti-ship missiles and surface-to-air missiles. This became what is now the dubbed anti-access, area denial (A2AD) concept to keep NATO naval and air power far from Russian key nuclear forces based on and the waters off the Peninsular.

The Russian Navy's next strategic mission is to provide naval forces for power-projection operations around the world, either providing naval battle groups or dispatching individual vessels on global flag-waving missions to support Russian diplomacy. Balancing the requirements for power-projection with protecting its strategic deterrent has long been a challenge for the Murmansk-based Northern Fleet.

The Northern Fleet suffered heavily in the 1990s as the overhaul and modernisation of its warships was repeatedly delayed and the purchase of replacement ships failed to get approval from the chaotic government of President Boris Yeltsin.

The early 1990s was a time of freefalling defence spending in Russia and the Northern Fleet struggled to bring RFS *Admiral Kuznetsov* fully into service. She only went to sea with a full air group in 1993. The carrier led a naval deployment to the Mediterranean in 1996 but the ship was dogged by mechanical problems during the cruise. Up to 2012 she made three more cruises to the Mediterranean but even these were not without problems and a sailor died in a major fire on the ship off the Turkish coast in 2009.

Russia's intervention in the Syrian conflict from 2015 prompted Moscow to begin preparing to dispatch the carrier and a naval battlegroup to the region. The force set sail in October 2016 and passed through the English Channel a few days later, prompting the British Defence Secretary ➤

LEFT: In 2017, the RFS *Admiral Kuznetsov* began a major upgrade and overhaul that is expected to finish later this year to allow the carrier to return to service with the Northern Fleet in 2025. (MIKHAIL ROGOV)

BELOW: After the PD-50 floating dock sank in October 2017 so the Russian Navy had to launch a project to build a dry dock to allow the RFS *Admiral Kuznetsov* to be taken out of the water, delaying the carriers overhaul. (MAXAR TECHNOLOGIES)

ABOVE: The Su-33 saw action for the first time in the ground attack role during the Russian intervention in Syria in November and December 2016. (RUSSIAN PRESIDENTIAL PRESS OFFICE)

Michael Fallon to call the carrier the 'Ship of Shame' because it seemed she was heading to take part in the Syrian conflict on the side of the Damascus government. On November 21, 2016, Su-33 jets from the ship carried out the first ever combat missions by Russian or Soviet carrier-borne aircraft when they launched bombing missions around the rebel-held city of Aleppo.

The mission was not without its problems, and faults in the ship's arrestor wires led to two jets, a Mikoyan MiG-29K (NATO: Fulcrum) and Su-33, being unable to land back on deck, forcing them to ditch.

Until the problem was resolved the air group temporarily relocated to a Russian-controlled air base in Syria to continue strike operations. In January 2017, the then commander of the Russian Group of Forces in Syria, Colonel-General Andrei Kartapolov, revealed that the Admiral Kuzentsov's jets flew 420 sorties during the ship's cruise in the Mediterranean. "Over the two months of their participation in combat operations, naval aviation pilots carried out 420 sorties, including 117 in nighttime, to attack 1,252 targets," he said.

Budget problems led to speculation that the ship might have to be

scrapped but in 2017 it was decided to begin a major upgrade. This was beset by technical problems.

Putting off the recapitalisation of the Northern Fleet's capital ships for two decades by delaying the building of a new aircraft carrier, came back to bite Moscow in October 2018 when the PD-50 floating dock at No 82 Ship Repair Yard at Roslyakovo, near Murmansk, sank as the RFS *Admiral Kuznetsov*, was being manoeuvred out after a refit period. As the 330-metre-long dock sank underneath the carrier, one of the PD-50's cranes toppled onto the deck of the RFS *Admiral Kuznetsov*. Although the damage to the carrier appeared to be only superficial the loss of the PD-50 created a major headache for the Northern Russian Navy. The dock was the only one in northern Russia that could take RFS *Admiral Kuznetsov* out of the water to carry out work on her hull, throwing into doubt whether the carrier will be ready to return to service. A plan was hatched to extend an existing dry dock at No 35 Shipyard in Murmansk to take the carrier. Further delay has been caused because of a dispute with contractors. The ship has now been moved out of the dry dock and the Russian Navy is claiming she will return to sea in 2024 and become operational again the following year.

In 2020 proposals were reportedly made to Russian President Vladimir Putin to begin work on a US-style super carrier but the high cost meant it was not taken up. The RFS *Admiral Kuznetsov* will have to soldier on for many years to come.

RIGHT: A blast deflector is raised before the launch of jets off from the RFS *Admiral Kuznetsov*. It protects aircraft and personnel in the rear section of the carrier's flight deck during fast jet launches. (RUSSIAN PRESIDENTIAL PRESS OFFICE)

Russian Naval Aviation

Naval Aviation is a distinct branch of the Russian Navy and each of the country's main regional fleets have its own aviation component. Fighter jets provide air defence of naval bases, strike jets are tasked to attack enemy warships, maritime patrol aircraft look for hostile submarines and operate anti-submarine and attack helicopters that are embarked on warships. Drones have started to be deployed to monitor sensitive sea zones.

Russia has a long naval aviation tradition stretching back into Soviet times, but it is only since the demise of the Soviet Union that supersonic fast jets have flown off aircraft carriers.

The Soviet Navy was on the brink of bringing the Sukhoi Su-33 (NATO: Flanker-D) into service when the Soviet Union collapsed, plunging the whole project into doubt. A naval aviation regiment had been formed at Saki airbase on Crimea in 1986 to begin training to operate the Su-33 when Ukraine broke away from the Soviet Union. The naval aviators opted to remain in the Russian Navy and relocated to an airbase of the Northern Fleet near the city of Severomorsk on the Kola Peninsula, which was to be the new home port of the RFS *Admiral Kuznetsov*.

The first deck landings on the carrier took place in 1991 and the ship deployed on its first operational cruise in 1996.

LEFT: Airborne early warning for the RFS *Admiral Kuznetsov* is provided by the Ka-31 and three are is service with the Russian Navy. (DMITRIY PICHUGIN)

The Northern Fleet Naval Aviation component is based at four airfields around Severomorsk. This includes the RFS *Admiral Kuznetsov's* air group of just over 30 Sukhoi Su-33 and Mikoyan MiG-29KR combat aircraft. Shore-based Su-24 bombers and MiG-31 fighters are also based south of the port city. A dozen or so Kamov Ka-27PL/PS anti-submarine, Ka-29 assault and Ka-31 early warning helicopters are available to deploy on Northern Fleet ships. To provide anti-submarine cover there are 10 classic configuration Iluyshin Il-38 maritime patrol aircraft and two Il-20T instrumented trial aircraft to support missile firings at test ranges around the Barents and White Seas. Logistic support is provided by a fleet of 10 Antonov An-26, Tupolov Tu-134 and Mil Mi-8.

Long-range maritime patrol support for the Northern Fleet is also provided by the 19 Tupolov Tu-142 turbo-prop maritime patrol aircraft based at Kipelovo airbase to the east of St Petersburg. Since 2017, the Northern Fleet has fielded its own regiment of Israeli-designed, but Russian- assembled IAI Forpost tactical unmanned aerial vehicles to support land and maritime operations.

Since Moscow's forces occupied Crimea in 2014, the Russian Navy has returned to Saki airbase and began to use it for practicing carrier landings and take-offs. A mock ski-jump has been installed and a runway is marked out to mimic the RFS *Admiral Kuznetsov's* deck so pilots practice operating from it.

BELOW LEFT: MiG-29K air defence and strike jets complete the RFS *Admiral Kuznetsov* air group. Like the Su-33, the MiG-20K is modified with folding wings to allow it to be moved below deck into the carrier's hanger. (ALAN WILSON)

BELOW RIGHT: The Su-33's pedigree can be traced back to classic land-based Su-27 fighter jet but the Russian Naval Aircraft is in need of a major upgrade to its weapon system and sensors. (CHRIS LOFTING)

ADMIRAL KUZNETSOV AIR GROUP, MAY 2024

Unit	Aircraft	Role	Home Base
100th Shipborne Fighter Aviation Regiment	MiG-29K/UBR	Strike/Air Defence	Severomorsk-3
279th Shipborne Fighter Aviation Regiment	Su-33, Su-25UTB	Strike/Air Defence	Severomorsk-3
830th Independent Shipborne Anti-Submarine Helicopter Regiment	Ka-29	Attack	Severomorsk-1
	Ka-31	Airborne Early Warning	
	Ka-52K	Attack	
	Ka-27PL/M	Anti-Submarine	
	Ka-27PS	Search and Rescue	

Armada Española

Spain's Carrier

Span's interest in aircraft carriers has its roots in the 1960s after the country allowed the United States to open air and naval bases on its territory. The Spanish government was very keen to join NATO and saw the development of military forces that would be attractive to the alliance as a way to help speed its membership bid.

The *Armada Española* saw the fielding of an aircraft carriers as a way to do this and opened negotiations with the US to secure the transfer of a surplus World War Two era Indepedennce-class light fleet carrier. The USS *Cabot* joined the *Armada Española* in 1967 as the SPS *Dédalo*. It was intended to form the core of an anti-submarine task group operating helicopters.

Once in service, the SPS *Dédalo* was also intended to transport marines during amphibious operations. Spanish defence strategy was evolving planning, and their marines were given the potential task of retaking the Canary and Azores Island chains if they were ever captured by Soviet amphibious assaults. This prompted interest in enhancing the capabilities of the SPS *Dédalo* to include fixed wing aviation to provide close air support to marines during beach assaults.

In the early 1970s the US Marine Corps was buying its first Hawker Siddeley AV-8B Harrier jump jets to operate from its amphibious ships and the Spanish looked to emulate them.

In 1972, Hawker Siddeley flew a Harrier to Spain to make a test landing on the SPS *Dédalo's* wooden flight deck. After the successful test, the US helped persuade the British to sell the *Armada Española* a batch Harriers, which they dubbed the AV-8S Matador. The aircraft were in operational service on SPS *Dédalo* in 1976, three years before the Royal Navy own Hawker Siddeley Sea Harrier FRS1s entered service on British aircraft carriers, making Spain the first European navy to operate a 'Harrier Carrier'.

Spain joined NATO in 1982 and since then its aircraft carriers have participated in numerous alliance exercises around the Mediterranean and Atlantic regions. The SPS *Dédalo* was replaced by the home-built SPS *Príncipe de Asturias* in 1988. She

RIGHT: Spanish AV-8A Matador jump jets went to sea on the SPS *Dédalo* in 1976 after successful trials in 1972. The Spanish navy was the first European navy to operate the iconic jump jet. (US NAVY)

BELOW: The SPS *Juan Carlos I* is now Spain's operational carrier but there are doubts about the long-term viability of its EAV-8B Matadors after the US Marine Corps retires its version of the jump jet in two years time. (JAVICASELLI)

embarked the upgraded EAV-8B Matador, essentially a McDonnell Douglas AV-8B Harrier II, and was fitted with ski-jump to enhance their operational performance.

The ship remained in service until 2012 when a new class of light carrier/amphibious assault ship entered service. The SPS *Juan Carlos I* was laid down in 2005 and was initially known as a Strategic Projection Vessel because of its multi-role capabilities. Her crew of 900 can be complemented by another 1,200 marines or passengers. The ship is based at Rota Naval Base at part Naval Action Group 2, which also includes Spain's amphibious landing ships. Her air wing is based nearby at Rota's military air base.

The Spanish Navy's remaining dozen or so EAV-8Bs are long due to be replaced but the Madrid government has put off making a decision on whether to buy the only viable option, the Lockheed Martin F-35B Lightning II jump jet. Italy and the United States Marine Corps will both retired their last AV-8Bs over the next two years, leaving Spain the only operator of the aircraft until its planned retirement in 2030.

There has been speculation that the Spanish government could soon decide to launch a major rearmament plan that would include the purchase of a batch of between 12 and 25 F-35Bs for the SPS *Juan Carlos I* but no official confirmation has emerged in public.

ABOVE: The SPS *Príncipe de Asturias* was Spain's first home-built aircraft carrier and the country's ship building industry used the experience to develop the Juan Carlos-class that has been exported as an aircraft carrier and amphibious assault ship. (US NAVY)

SPANISH NAVAL AVIATION (ARMA AEREA DE LA ARMADA ESPANOLA), MAY 2024			
Squadron	Type	Role	Home Base
003 Escuadrilla	AB212+	ASW/AEW	NAS Rota
005 Escuadrilla	SH-60F	ASW/AEW	NAS Rota
009 Escuadrilla	EAV-8B/EAV-8B+/TAV-8B Matador II	Strike Air Defence	NAS Rota
010 Escuadrilla	SH-60B/F Seahawk	ASW/AEW	NAS Rota

LEFT: The SPS *Juan Carlos I* now usually deployed with an air group of EAV-8Bs and anti-submarine helicopters. (US NAVY)

Turkey Goes Unmanned

UAV Carrier Force

Turkey has major ambitions for its naval forces and has been investing heavily in new shipping. The new pride of the Turkish navy is the TCG *Anadolu*, which was commissioned into the fleet in April 2023. She is a derivative of the Spanish Juan Carlos I-class light aircraft carrier/ amphibious assault ship and is destined to be the world's first dedicated unmanned aerial vehicle (UAV) carrier.

Construction began at Sedef Shipbuilding in Istanbul in 2016 with a Turkish-Spanish consortium overseeing the project. Turkish-supplied electronics and other major systems are installed on the ship.

The vessel is intended to undertake long-endurance, long-distance military combat or humanitarian relief operations around the Mediterranean and Black Sea regions, while acting as a command centre and flagship for the Turkish Navy. Over the past two decades Turkey has carried out non-combatant evacuation operations in Libya and dispatched intervention forces to the North African country on a number of occasions. It has ambitions to be able to influence events far from its home waters and is already planning the construction of a sister ship to the TCG *Anadolu,* named TCG *Trakya*. This would give the Turks the ability to sustain long term deployments of light aircraft carriers.

The arrival of the TCG *Anadolu* expanded dramatically Turkey's naval capability, which up to then did not have a dedicated platform to operate helicopters. Up to 20 helicopters can operate from the new ship and the Turkish navy has ambitions to fly strike drones off her to support amphibious operations.

Initial plans called for the ship to be Turkey's first every aircraft carrier but a dispute of with the United States over the purchase of Lockheed Martin F-35B Lightning II fighter jets meant a new approach was needed. The Turkish Navy announced the TCG *Anadolu* would operate a mix of UAVs and helicopters. This would

make the Turkey the first nation to operate an aircraft carrier with UAVs as its primary offensive aircraft. The Turkish aviation company, Baykar Defense, set to designing and building a family of UAVs to operate off the TCG *Anadolu*. The company has already built armed UAVs that have seen action in Syria, Libya, Ukraine and Nagorno-Karabakh.

The first UAV to see service on the TCG *Anadolu,* is designated the Bayraktar TB3, which flew for the first time in October 2023. It has folding wings, can land on an aircraft carrier and can carry heavy guided munitions. This is a derivative of the TB2 which has seen extensive combat service in several war zones.

TB3 is designed to operate alongside Bayraktar Kızılelma, which is powered by a jet engine and is intended to penetrate into heavily defended airspace. The TB3 is a medium altitude, long endurance (MALE) class UAV and is intended to operate in more benign environments or collect intelligence from stand-off distances so it does not have to expose itself to enemy air defences.

DENİZ KUVVETLERİ KOMUTANLIĞI DİZAYN PROJE OFİSİ MÜDÜRLÜĞÜ

GENEL KARAKTERİSTİKLER
TAM BOY : 285 M
GENİŞLİK : 72 M
SU ÇEKİMİ : 10.1 M
DEPLASMAN : 60000 TON
HIZ : 25 KNOTS
ANA TAHRİK SİSTEMİ : COGAG (4 x G/T)
UÇAK KALKIŞ/İNİŞ SİSTEMİ : STOBAR

GEMİ TASARIMINDA TAM VE MİLLİ KABİLİYET

LEFT: Turkey is now looking to build a purposed designed 60,000-ton aircraft carrier to operate a mix of manned jets and drones. (@er_tugay)

The Bayraktar Kızılelma, or Red Apple, is a single-engine, low-observable carrier-capable combat UAV. The initial Bayraktar Kızılelma, known as Kızılelma-A, is subsonic. Subsequent variants, the Kızılelma-B and Kızılelma-C, are intended to be supersonic, the latter having a twin-engined configuration.

Other nations, including the United States, have experimented with flying UAVs onto aircraft carriers but the Turkish Navy is the first naval force to commit to deploying these new weapons on its warships as a matter of routine.

BELOW: The Bayraktar Kızılelma combat drone is next in line to operate from the TCG *Anadolu*. (ATA BARIS)

UK Carrier Strike Group

Back in the Carrier Game

HMS *Queen Elizabeth* and HMS *Prince of Wales* are at the core of the United Kingdom Carrier Strike Group (UKCSG). One of the aircraft carriers, as well as their supporting warships and air group, are held at high readiness in Portsmouth ready to scramble to protect British interests around the world.

The former commander of the Carrier Strike Group (UKCSG), Commodore Steve Moorhouse, described it as the "embodiment of British maritime power, and sits at the heart of a modernised and emboldened Royal Navy.

"Protected by a ring of advanced destroyers, frigates, helicopters and submarines, and equipped with fifth generation fighters, HMS *Queen Elizabeth* is able to strike from the sea at a time and place of our choosing; and with our NATO allies at our side, we will be ready to fight and win in the most demanding circumstances," he said. "Carrier Strike offers

Britain choice and flexibility on the global stage; it reassures our friends and allies and presents a powerful deterrent to would-be adversaries."

The current commander of the UKCSG, Commodore James Blackmore, and his twenty strong staff are based in Portsmouth when not at sea on their flagship. They are responsible for organising and training the carrier strike group before missions and they take command of all its warships and aircraft when it sails from Portsmouth.

UKCSG existed in various forms since the mid-2000s and underwent a major change in 2006 when the last Hawker Siddeley Sea Harrier FA2 air supremacy fighters were retired. The UK's Joint Force Harrier then transitioned to solely operating the BAE Systems Harrier GR9 strike jet, which was optimised for attacking land targets with precision guided weapons. This marked the full transition of the Royal Navy's Invincible-class carriers from ships optimised for fleet action at sea into strike carriers focused on projecting air power ashore. In the 2010 the Strategic Defence and Security Review the Invincible-class carriers and the Harriers were retired, leaving a 'carrier gap' until HMS *Queen Elizabeth* put to sea in June 2017.

The UKCSG staff reformed in 2015 to bring the Queen Elizabeth-class carriers into service and regenerate the Royal Navy's naval aviation capability. Following Exercise Joint

Warrior 2021, the UKCSG reached its initial operating capability (IOC) milestone in January 2021. This milestone marked the successful operation of all components of the CSG into a single integrated force, which was available for operational deployments. Four months later HMS *Queen Elizabeth* sailed to the Far East for the Carrier Strike Group 2021 deployment.

The Royal Navy firmly describes the Queen Elizabeth-class ships as strike carriers, and they are trained primarily to project airpower ashore in variety of scenarios. Their main aircraft, the Lockheed Martin F-35B Lightning II, jump jet is optimised for strike missions against heavily defended land targets, rather than air defence or maritime attack against enemy fleets. Currently a squadron »

ABOVE: The flight deck of the Queen Elizabeth-class aircraft carriers overhangs the side of the ship's hull. (MOD/CROWNCOPYRIGHT)

LEFT: Type 23 frigates are an essential part of the Royal Navy escorts that protect Britain's aircraft carriers. (MOD/CROWNCOPYRIGHT)

ABOVE: Flying the flag. HMS *Prince of Wales* led the NATO carrier strike group during Exercise Steadfast Defender in February and March 2024. (MOD/CROWNCOPYRIGHT)

of F-35Bs, with up to 10 aircraft, are usually embarked on British carriers. When the second British F-35B squadron is declared fully operational in 2025, it is expected that both units, 617 Squadron of the RAF and 809 Naval Air Squadron, will embark for carrier deployments with 12 jets each.

British F-35Bs are currently only armed with the ASRAAM short range dogfighting missile and the Enhanced Paveway IV guided bomb. The jets are in theory, cleared to carry and fire the AIM-120 AMRAAM beyond visual range missile but this is rarely used as they take up too much room in the aircraft's weapon bay.

The internal design of the Queen Elizabeth-class carriers are optimised to generate strike sorties by rapidly turning around jets between missions, reloading them with bombs

and launching them back into the air. Britain's F-35Bs are jointly operated by the Royal Air Force and Royal Navy, which has prompted both services to work to establish new command arrangements for their employment of the aircraft when they are embarked on aircraft carriers. The RAF and Royal Navy envisage, that their carrier air power will be closely integrated with shore-based aircraft and other allied air forces. During major coalition or allied missions, the operation commander is likely to be a coalition air commander working at a shore-based combined air operations centre (CAOC).

Carrier-based British air assets allocated to participating in an air campaign are to be directed from the coalition CAOC on the air tasking order.

Any major national UK operations are expected to be run by a joint commander from a joint force headquarters, who will designate a joint force air component commander (JFACC), drawing on personnel from the RAF and Royal Navy to work in his headquarters. The location of the JFACC and his staff will be determined by the scenario. It is not necessarily the case that the air commander will be on the UK carrier.

The UKCSG battle staff can currently be expanded to enable it to act as an embarked JFACC on the British carriers, which have the space and the necessary communications links to accommodate an air planning staff if required. Communications feeds to allow staff on the ship to view imagery from General Atomics MQ-9 Reaper unmanned aerial vehicles and other surveillance aircraft are installed on the ships. RAF Air Command has its own deployable JFACC headquarters team that could embark on a carrier if necessary.

To defend its carriers, the Royal Navy usually provides a mix of warships, nuclear-powered submarines and support ships, as well as embarked helicopters. Air defence is usually provided by at least one Type 45 destroyer, which are equipped with Samson radar and armed with the long-range Aster surface-to-air missiles. Radar coverage of the CSG is extended by the airborne early warning variant of AgustaWestland Merlin HM2 helicopter equipped with the Crowsnest radar.

BELOW: The Queen Elizabeth-class carriers are designed to operate the F-35B Lightning II jump jets. (MOD/CROWNCOPYRIGHT)

Considerable resources are assigned to defend the carriers against hostile submarines. At least one Type 23 frigate, equipped with a towed array sonar, provides long range underwater surveillance to give early warning of the approach of submarines. A squadron of Merlin HM2 are usually embarked on British carriers to augment the anti-submarine screen of the CSG, hunting for submarines with their dipping sonar or sonobuoys.

The protection of CSG from surface threats is the responsibility of Leonardo Wildcat HMA2 maritime helicopters, embarked on the carrier or escorting warships. These helicopters are armed with Marlet short range missiles or the longer-range Sea Venom.

The final combat element of British CSGs are nuclear-powered Astute submarines. They have an important role in keeping enemy submarines away from the carriers but can also contribute to strike operations with their Tomahawk land attack missiles that can hit targets up 1,700 kilometres away.

The most recent UK CSG deployment occurred in February and March 2024, when HMS *Prince of Wales* took part in NATO's Exercise Steadfast Defender off the coast of Norway. The carrier is due to begin a period of work up training before sailing to the Far East next year for the Carrier Strike Group (CSG) 2025 deployment. Both 617 Squadron and 809 NAS are earmarked to embark for this deployment with a total of 24 jets to confirm the full operating capability of the UK carrier strike capability.

ABOVE: HMS *Queen Elizabeth* **'s flight deck is now ready to receive aircraft.** (TIM RIPLEY)

BELOW: HMS *Queen Elizabeth* **prepares to sail from Rosyth Dockyard.** (TIM RIPLEY)

Wings of the Fleet

British Carrier Airpower

RIGHT: RAF Marham in Suffolk is the home base of the British Lightning Force. (MOD/CROWNCOPYRIGHT)

BELOW: Test to expand the operating envelope of British F-35Bs to carry an array of precision guided munitions took place on HMS *Prince of Wales* in November 2023. (MOD/CROWNCOPYRIGHT)

Britain's Fleet Air Arm has pioneered in the development of carrier airpower for more than 100 years, so it is an organisation that has not been afraid to innovate to keep ahead of its opponents.

The Lockheed Martin F-35B Lightning II jump jet is Britain's current carrier-borne fixed wing aircraft, and they are operated in conjunction with the Royal Air Force.

The jets and personnel, drawn from the Royal Air Force and Royal Navy, are all part of the Lightning Force, or LF, which is home based at RAF Marham in Suffolk. It is currently focused on generating aircraft, aircrew and ground support personnel to provide the air groups for the two Queen Elizabeth-class aircraft carriers.

All parts of the LF are jointly manned by personnel from the two services, rather than operating as distinct RAF or RN units. Currently there is one fully operational F-35B unit, the famous 617 'Dambusters' Squadron, and an operational conversion unit, 207 Squadron. These are both RAF badged units.

From December 2023, a second operational unit, 809 Naval Air Squadron (NAS), began to form and

it is scheduled to be declared fully operational by the end of 2025. The training and operations of the LF are closely synchronised with the sailing programme of the aircraft carriers and it is now routine for 617 Squadron to deploy for at least one extended cruise on one of the carriers each year.

A major focus is on generating aircrew who have the necessary qualifications to fly off and land on aircraft carriers, so each year student pilots from 207 Squadron undertake short deployments on board one of the carriers cruising in UK waters.

It is intended that the RAF will take delivery of all 48 of its initial batch of F-35Bs by the end of 2025 and this is leading to an increase in training to build up enough instructors and student pilots to allow 809 NAS to become fully operational. It had been intended to form 809 NAS in April 2023, but this slipped and there had also been a delay in building its dedicated facilities at RAF Marham.

809 NAS traces its history back to 1941 when it was formed to fly the Fairy Fulmar attack aircraft. Flying the de Havilland Sea Venom it saw action in the 1956 Suez conflict and in the 1960s it converted to fly the iconic Blackburn Buccaneer S1 strike jet. It operated the Hawker Siddeley Sea Harrier FRS1 briefly during the 1982 Falkland war when several of its pilots joined the task force that

eventually recaptured the British islands. As a result of its badge, it is known as the 'Phoenix Squadron' and its pilots are nicknamed 'The Immortals'. It was reformed nearly 41 years to the day that it was disbanded at RNAS Yeovilton.

The final element of the LF is 17 Squadron, which is based at Edwards Air Force Base in California, and it is the UK's contribution to the US-led F-35 testing task force. Up until the end of 2023 three UK aircraft remained in the US to support testing but a fourth aircraft was then assigned to 17 Squadron straight from

the Fort Worth production line in Texas, without having been stationed at RAF Marham.

By early 2024, 35 F-35Bs had been handed over to the UK by Lockheed Martin. One had been lost in an accident in December 2021 during a take-off from HMS *Queen Elizabeth* in Mediterranean. This leaves 30 currently at the Norfolk base, operating with the LF.

Production problems with the latest variant of the F-35, the TR-3, has led to a block on all deliveries, which is impacting on the handing over of the last 13 UK jets. Lockheed Martin »

ABOVE: The Merlin HM2 hunts for submarines with its dipping sonar. (ROYAL NAVY, VIA LEONARDO)

RIGHT: Merlin HM2 are deployed from RNAS Culdrose to a variety of Royal Navy warships, including Type 23 frigates. (MOD/CROWNCOPYRIGHT)

are now not expecting deliveries to start until late 2024 at the earliest, putting in doubt the build up of the LF to its full strength ahead of the sailing of HMS *Prince of Wales* for CSG 25 next spring.

The next most important carrier-borne asset is the AgustaWestland Merlin HM2 maritime helicopter, which is operated by three Royal Navy squadrons, based at RNAS Culdrose in Cornwall.

814 Naval Air Squadron reformed in 2001 to operate the then new Merlin HM1 and subsequently re-equipped with upgraded Merlin HM2 in 2014. Personnel from the disbanded 829 Naval Air Squadron were incorporated into the unit in 2018, and 814 Squadron took over its role to supply independent flights on frigates and destroyers, as well as operating in the shore-based anti-submarine role from Prestwick International Airport in Scotland to protect Royal Navy nuclear deterrent submarines transiting to their home port at Faslane on the Clyde. It is nicknamed the 'Flying Tigers'.

820 Naval Air Squadron is now the core helicopter squadron for HMS *Queen Elizabeth's* air group, hence her nickname, 'The Queen's Squadron'. The squadron embarked on the carrier for her maiden operational Carrier Strike Group deployment to the Far East in 2021. It will transfer to HMS *Prince of Wales* when she takes over the role of fleet flagship in late 2024 ahead of the Carrier Strike Group 2025 deployment to the Far East

824 Naval Air Squadron was reformed in 2000 and it initially provided helicopters to operate as independent flights on frigates and destroyers. The unit's Merlins were named after knights of King Arthur's famous round table. It is now the main Merlin training unit, preparing pilots, observers, aircrew and grounds crew to operate the helicopter in a dedicated training facility at RNAS Culdrose that is equipped with purpose-built simulators.

UK CARRIER AIR GROUP, MAY 2024			
Unit	Aircraft	Home Base	Role
Royal Air Force			
617 Squadron	F-35B Lightning	RAF Marham	Carrier-borne fighter/strike
Fleet Air Arm			
809 Naval Air Squadron	F-35B Lightning	RAF Marham	Carrier-borne fighter/strike
814 Naval Air Squadron	Merlin HM2	RNAS Culdrose	Anti-submarine warfare/small ship flight
815 Naval Air Squadron	Wildcat HMA2	RNAS Yeovilton	Small ship flights
820 Naval Air Squadron	Merlin HM2	RNAS Culdrose	Anti-submarine warfare/carrier air group
824 Naval Air Squadron	Merlin HM2	RNAS Culdrose	Conversion Training
825 Naval Air Squadron	Wildcat HMA2	RNAS Yeovilton	Conversion Training
845 Naval Air Squadron	Merlin HC4A/HC4	RNAS Yeovilton	Medium lift

The Royal Navy Wildcat Force is home based at Royal Naval Air Station Yeovilton in Somerset and comprises two flying squadrons. 815 NAS provides flights of one or two of the 28 Leonardo Wildcat HMA2 maritime variants to be embarked on Royal Navy frigates, destroyers and carriers. Wildcat crews are trained to fly the helicopters by instructors from 825 NAS.

Logistic support or vertical replenishment helicopters are provided by 845 NAS at Yeovilton, which flies the Merlin HC4 Commando variant of the helicopters. They fly utility missions around the CSG, moving people and stores between ships. A key job for these helicopters is to fly personnel recovery or combat search and rescue (CSAR) missions to bring down F-35B pilots back to safety if they are lost over enemy territory.

The Royal Navy regularly welcomes RAF and Army Air Corps helicopters onto its aircraft carriers to exploit their unique capabilities. RAF Boeing Chinook HC5/6/6b heavy lift helicopters are called onto the carriers when large outsize cargoes are needed to be moved. British Army Boeing AH-6E Apache attack helicopters can provide additional strike capabilities, particularly when the carriers are supporting amphibious landings by Royal Marine Commandos.

ABOVE: The Mojave medium altitude, long endurance (MALE) unmanned aerial vehicle successfully landed and took off from HMS *Prince of Wales* in November 2023. (MOD/CROWNCOPYRIGHT)

LEFT: The jet powered Banshee drone has been test launched from HMS *Prince of Wales*. (MOD/CROWNCOPYRIGHT)

LEFT: Royal Navy Merlin HM2 maritime helicopters provide anti-submarine protection for Britain's two Queen Elizabeth-class aircraft carriers. (MOD/CROWNCOPYRIGHT)

US Carrier Fleets

Bring on the Super Carriers

RIGHT: US Navy aircraft carriers accommodate an 'air force in a box' on their flight decks to allow air power to be projected into crisis zones around the world. (US NAVY)

FAR RIGHT: The 5th generation F-35C Lightning II is starting to appear on the decks of US aircraft carriers to transform the strike power of their air wings. (US NAVY)

US NAVY CARRIERS AND ASSAULT SHIPS, MAY 2024				
Nimitz-Class	Ship	Commissioned	Home Port (Fleet)	Status/Location May 2024
CVN-68	USS Nimitz	03-May-75	Bremerton, Washington (Pacific)	To deploy in late 2024
CVN-69	USS Dwight D. Eisenhower	18-Oct-77	Norfolk, Virginia (Atlantic)	Mediterranean
CVN-70	USS Carl Vinson	13-Mar-82	San Diego, California (Pacific)	West Pacific
Theodore Roosevelt Sub-Class				
CVN-71	USS Theodore Roosevelt	25-Oct-86	San Diego, California (Pacific)	South China Sea
CVN-72	USS Abraham Lincoln	11-Nov-89	San Diego, California (Pacific)	To deploy in late 2024
CVN-73	USS George Washington	04-Jul-92	Yokosuka, Japan (from late 2024) (Pacific)	South America, sailing to Yokosuka, Japan
CVN-74	USS John C. Stennis	09-Dec-95	Norfolk, Virginia (Atlantic)	Refuel and overhaul until 3rd quarter 2025
CVN-75	USS Harry S. Truman	25-Jul-98	Norfolk, Virginia (Atlantic)	North Atlantic, refuel/overhaul in 2026
Ronald Reagan Sub-Class				
CVN-76	USS Ronald Reagan	12-Jul-03	Yokosuka, Japan (Pacific) (return to CONUS 2024)	West Pacific
CVN-77	USS George H.W. Bush	10-Jan-09	Norfolk, Virginia (Atlantic)	Maintenance in Norfolk until July 2024
Ford Class				
CVN-78	USS Gerald R. Ford	22-Jul-17	Norfolk, Virginia (Atlantic)	post deployment maintenance in Norfolk
CVN-79	USS John F. Kennedy	2025	Huntington Ingalls Industries' Newport News, Virginia	Fitting out
CVN-80	USS Enterprise	2028	Huntington Ingalls Industries' Newport News, Virginia	Under construction
CVN-81	USS Doris Miller	2032	Huntington Ingalls Industries' Newport News, Virginia	Under construction
CVN-82	not yet named	2036	Huntington Ingalls Industries' Newport News, Virginia	Ordered
Wasp-Class				
LHD-1	USS Wasp	29-Jul-89	Norfolk, Virginia (Atlantic)	Sea trials after maintenance
LHD-2	USS Essex	17-Oct-92	San Diego, California (Pacific)	Maintenance until Dec 2024
LHD-3	USS Kearsarge	16-Oct-93	Norfolk, Virginia (Atlantic)	Maintenance until Nov 2024
LHD-4	USS Boxer	11-Feb-95	San Diego, California (Pacific)	San Diego, to deploy May 2024?
LHD-5	USS Bataan	20-Sep-97	Norfolk, Virginia (Atlantic)	Post deployment recovery period
LHD-6	USS Bonhomme Richard	15-Aug-98	San Diego, California (Pacific)	To be sold for scrap after accidental fire
LHD-7	USS Iwo Jima	30-Jun-01	Norfolk, Virginia (Atlantic)	Maintenance
LHD-8	USS Makin Island	24-Oct-09	San Diego, California (Pacific)	Maintenance period until Oct 2024
America-Class				Status
Flight 0				
LHA-6	USS America	11-Oct-14	Sasebo, Nagasaki (Pacific)	South China Sea
LHA-7	USS Tripoli	15-Jul-20	San Diego, California (Pacific)	Sea trials after maintenance
Flight I				
LHA-8	USS Bougainville	Late 2024	Ingalls Shipbuilding, Pascagoula, Mississippi	Under construction
LHA-9	USS Fallujah	2029-30?	Ingalls Shipbuilding, Pascagoula, Mississippi	Under construction
LHA-10	USS Helmand Province		Ingalls Shipbuilding, Pascagoula, Mississippi	Authorized

America boasts the world's largest force of aircraft carriers, which currently stand at 10 Nimitz-class ships and one Gerald R Ford-class nuclear-powered ship, as well as nine smaller amphibious assault ships that can operate US Marine Corps strike jets.

These ships are grouped under the command of several different fleets, naval tasks forces and strike groups. US Navy carriers and amphibious ships are switched, or 'chopped', between the command of these organisations depending on whether they are undergoing maintenance, training or participating in live operations.

The US Navy operates its aircraft carriers in what is known as a 'force generation cycle', which see them move through periods of maintenance, training and then operations under the command of what are termed 'geographical combatant commanders' in the North Atlantic, European, the Middle East and Western Pacific regions.

Force generation of carriers and their aircraft are the responsibility of the specific commands on the Pacific and Atlantic coasts. The Naval Air Force Pacific controls seven aircraft carriers and their supporting air wings. The Naval Air Force Atlantic, has the same function on the US Eastern seaboard, with the remaining four carriers and their assigned air wings. These two commands have the responsibility for generating trained sailors and aviators to serve on the ships and then getting the carriers ready to deploy to operational theatres. When ships come out of maintenance, their crews are put through intense training exercises to get them ready for the challenges they will face during upcoming deployments.

Prior to sailing, ships and air wings are grouped into what are designated 'carrier strike groups', or CSG, under the command of a rear admiral. Strike groups combine an aircraft carrier and its air wing, as well as a supporting surface squadron of cruisers, destroyers and frigates, as well as a nuclear-powered attack submarines and supply ships. CSGs staff are usually kept in

existence for several years while an aircraft carrier is operational, so the command staff and assigned ships can get used to working with each other.

Once a CSG sails from port they conduct a "CHange of OPerational control", known 'chopping', and the regional combatant command brings them under control. Each combatant command has its own air, land and naval component command, with the latter usually being a numbered US Navy fleet. These number fleets are organised around a series of task forces, which control their main operational elements, such as aircraft carriers, surface vessels, maritime patrol aircraft, submarines and logistic support assets.

So, when a CSG arrives in an operational theatre, its aircraft carrier, air wing and several escort vessels are re-designated the carrier task force for that region. Other elements of the CSG can be assigned to surface or logistic task forces, depending on the operational situation.

US Navy carrier task forces rarely operate on their own and are integrated into their regional combatant commander's battle plans. For example, all air operations over land are the responsibility of the regional air component command, which are usually led by US Air Force officers based in a combined air operations centre, or CAOC. These are high-tech command posts that have real-time intelligence feeds showing all air movements in operational theatres. Any US Navy aircraft that are assigned to strike at land targets are directed by the CAOC, according to a daily air tasking order. If USAF aircraft are assigned to attack enemy ships at sea, the US Navy would control their operations. To co-ordinate this division of command, senior officers from air wings are dispatched to the USAF CAOCs whenever a CSG arrives in operational theatre.

Similar command arrangements are put in place for amphibious landing ships and their embarked US Marine Corps aviation units. Amphibious assault ships and supporting dock landing ships are termed an 'amphibious ready group', or ARG. When supporting surface warships, maritime patrol aircraft, logistic support ships and submarines are attached for bigger missions, they are designed as Expeditionary Strike Groups, or ESG. As with CSGs, whenever ARGs or ESGs arrive in operational theatres they are usually re-designated as task forces under a numbered fleet's command.

LEFT: Norfolk Naval Station in Virginia is home to the Atlantic coast-based aircraft carriers. In 2012, five carriers - USS *Dwight D Eisenhower*, USS *George HW Bush*, USS *Enterprise*, USS *Harry S Truman*, and USS *Abraham Lincoln* - were tied up on 'carrier row'. (US NAVY)

LEFT: Each US Navy aircraft carrier provides 4.5 acres of sovereign territory that can be manoeuvred around the world's ocean to allow American presidents to intervene in crisis or wars. (US NAVY)

LEFT: America's aircraft carriers are controlled by six US Navy numbered fleets that are responsible for specific regions of the world. (US NAVY)

3F 2F 6F 5F 7F 4F

US Pacific Fleet

Carriers Dominate

ABOVE: When the Chinese navy put to sea in the autumn of 2023 to conduct exercises around Taiwan the Pentagon dispatched the USS *Carl Vinson* to the Western Pacific. (US NAVY)

America has long used its aircraft carriers to project military power in the Pacific region, stretching back to the days of the island-hopping campaign against Imperial Japan in World War Two. In the Cold War era, US aircraft carriers launched air strikes against Communist forces in Korea, Vietnam, Laos and Cambodia. It was also commonplace for aircraft carriers to be dispatched whenever regional allies, such as Taiwan and South Korea, were threatened by hostile powers.

The US Navy's Pacific Fleet was at the heart of all these operations from its headquarters at Pearl Harbor on the Hawaiian island of Oahu. In World War Two, the US Navy controlled the Pacific theatre of operations but in the 1950s, the US military set up the first of what were called at the time unified commands, with air, navy and land component commands. This eventually led to the establishment of Pacific Command (PACOM), with its headquarters at Camp HM Smith, close to Pearl Harbor. A US Navy four-star admiral has always been commander of PACOM after it was first established in 1947.

In 2018, PACOM was renamed Indo-Pacific Command (INDOPACOM) to reflect the growing importance of the Indian Ocean region, even through

PACOM had been responsible for the US naval operations in much of the Indian Ocean since the 1970s. INDOPACOM's headquarters remained at Camp HM Smith in Hawaii.

The US Pacific Fleet is now the naval component of INDOPACOM, and it uniquely has two numbered fleets under its command. The Seventh Fleet has its headquarters in Japan and controls all naval operations in the Western Pacific region and the Third Fleet at San Diego controls naval operations off the US western seaboard, along Alaska's coast and out into the Pacific around the Hawaiian Islands.

Aircraft carriers remain central to US operations in the Indo-Pacific theatre but the days of fleets of carriers based at Pearl Harbor or Subic Bay in the Philippines are a thing of the past. The huge cost of operating nuclear-powered aircraft carriers has forced the US Navy to concentrate them at fewer naval bases to make maintenance more efficient and reduce costs. It also reduces disruption to sailors and their families.

The Pacific Fleet now has three main ports for its carriers. One carrier is forward deployed in Japan at Yokosuka, another is at Bremerton in Washington State, and the remaining five are home ported at San Diego. These naval bases have the facilities to perform routine maintenance and limited upgrades to carriers and their systems. However, refuelling and complex overhauls, or RCOH, can now only be carried out at Newport News Shipbuilding in Norfolk, Virginia.

Since 2018, the US Navy has moved to what is dubbed the 'dynamic force employment' model which envisages keeping carrier strike groups at readiness near their home port and only surging them forward in times of crisis. This reduces wear and tear on ships and aircraft, as well as helping to limit the time sailors have to spend away from their families, improving retention.

The Pacific Fleet's naval air squadrons are located at several air bases along the Western seaboard, except for those assigned to the

RIGHT: Pacific Fleet aircraft carriers are starting to go to sea with the 5th generation F-35C Lightning II in their air groups. (US NAVY)

US CARRIER STRIKE GROUPS IN PACIFIC FLEET, MAY 2024						
Carrier Strike Group	CSG-1	CSG-5	CSG-3	CSG-9	CSG-11	Unassigned
Location	San Diego, CA	Yokosuka, Japan	San Diego, CA	South China Sea	Bremerton, WA	US Southern Command AOR (en route to Japan)
Aircraft Carrier (CVN)	USS Carl Vinson (CVN 70)	USS Ronald Reagan (CVN 76)	USS Abraham Lincoln (CVN 72)	USS Theodore Roosevelt (CVN 71)	USS Nimitz (CVN 78)	USS George Washington (CVN 73)
Carrier Air Group (CVW)	*CVW 2*	*CVW 5*	*CVW 9*	*CVW 11*	*CVW 17*	*CVW7*
Ticonderoga-class cruisers	USS Princeton (CG-59)	USS Chancellorsville (CG-62)	USS Mobile Bay (CG-53)	USS Lake Erie (CG-70)	USS Bunker Hill (CG-52)	
		USS Antietam (CG-54)				
		USS Robert Smalls (CG-62)				
Destroyer Squadron	*DESRON-1*	*DESRON-15*	*DESRON-21*	*DESRON-23*	*DESRON-9*	
Arleigh Burke-class destroyer	USS Hopper (DDG-70)	USS Benfold (DDG-65)	USS Fitzgerald (DDG-62)	USS John S. McCain (DDG-56)	USS Decatur (DDG-73)	USS Porter (DDG-78)
	USS Kidd (DDG-100)	USS Milius (DDG-69)	USS Gridley (DDG- 101)	USS Halsey (DDG-97)	USS Paul Hamilton (DDG-60)	
	USS Sterett (DDG 104)	USS Higgins (DDG-76)	USS Sampson (DDG-102)	USS Daniel Inouye (DDG-118)	USS Chung Hoon (DDG-93)	
	USS William P. Lawrence (DDG 110)	USS Howard (DDG-83)	USS Spruance (DDG-111)		USS Wayne E. Meyer (DDG-108)	
		USS McCampbell (DDG-85)			USS Shoup (DDG-86)	
		USS Shoup (DDG-86)				
		USS Dewey (DDG-105)				
		USS John Finn (DDG-113)				
		USS Ralph Johnson (DDG-114)				
		USS Rafael Peralta (DDG-115)				
Date of Deployment and CSG composition	Oct-23	Apr-23	mid 2023	Apr-24	2023	

Note all above vessels are home ported in Japan under CSG-5, with up four ships sailing in each deployment

FAR LEFT: The Pacific has been the main venue for US Navy aircraft carriers since World War Two when its flat tops duelled with those of Imperial Japan. The USS *Yorktown* in a dry dock at the Pearl Harbor Naval Shipyard in May 1942. (US NATIONAL ARCHIVE)

LEFT: The USS *Ronald Reagan* and her supporting warships are forward based in Japan to provide the 7th Fleet with its own integral carrier strike group. (US NAVY)

forward based carrier, which are based at Marine Corps Air Station (MCAS) Iwakuni in Japan. Major training exercises and test firing of aircraft weapons takes place at the Point Mugu test range on the Pacific coast and Naval Air Station (NAS) Fallon in Nevada. Carrier air wings carry out intense training at these sites in their work-up periods, prior to sailing on operational cruises.

US Seventh Fleet

Tip of the Spear

From its headquarters at US Fleet Activities site in Yokosuka, in Japan, the US Seventh Fleet controls US naval operations across more that 124 million squares of ocean, stretching from the International Date Line, west of Hawaii to the India/Pakistan border and from the Kuril Islands in the North to the Antarctic in the South. Its area of operations encompasses 36 maritime countries and 50% of the world's population.

The Seventh Fleet is the largest US Navy's forward-deployed fleets and at any given time there are 50-70 ships and submarines, 150 aircraft, and more than 27,000 Sailors and Marines are under its command.

It is the only forward deployed numbered fleet to have its own aircraft carrier and support air wing home based in its operational area. This is currently the USS *Ronald Reagan* but, during late 2024/early 2025, she is scheduled to swop over with the USS *George Washington*, which has recently completed a ROCH period and it is currently undergoing a workup cruise.

The Yokosuka-based carrier is assigned to Carrier Strike Group 5 (CSG-5) and when at sea on operations it is designated Task Force 70. This designation passes to other carriers that come under command of the Seventh Fleet and if two carrier strike groups are present, then they become Task Force 70.1 and 70.2, respectively. The nine squadrons of Carrier Air Wing 5 are based at MCAS Iwakuni in Japan and they usually embark on which ever carrier is home ported in Yokosuka.

US Marine Corps amphibious forces based in Japan and on the island of Okinawa come under the command of the Seventh Fleet's Task Force 76, when they are deployed at sea. The core of Task Force 76 is the USS *America* and its Amphibious Ready Group (ARG) of dock landing ships, which are home part at Sasebo in southern Japan. They are ready to embark 2,200 marines and supporting aircraft and helicopters of the 31st Marine Expeditionary Unit (MEU).

America's growing rivalry with China and the threat to South Korea from North Korea has resulted in the Western Pacific being a key strategic region for the US Navy. As a result, it has aimed to keep at least one carrier strike group at sea in the Seventh Fleet area of responsibility at all times, as well as an amphibious ready group. A six-month long rotation schedule ensures than one of the east coast-home ported carriers is in the Western Pacific on a continuous basis and the Japan-based carrier is held at readiness to be surged to sea in time of crisis or for major fleet exercises.

In first half of 2024, Task Force 70's carrier at sea was USS *Theodore Roosevelt* after she replaced USS *Carl Vinson* at the start of the year. The low availability of amphibious ships has meant that a similar rotation has not been possible to establish, and the Japan-based USS *America* has had to pull more sea duty. She is set to be replaced in the Western Pacific later in the summer by USS *Boxer* and her ARG, but USS *Boxer* was delayed because of technical problems.

The immediate focus of US naval operations in the Western Pacific is ensuring freedom of navigation in waters claimed by China, resulting in a series of confrontation with the vessels and aircraft of Beijing's navy. Tension with China over Taiwan are not new but that have reached new levels in recent years.

US aircraft carriers have always played a key role in these operations, but the expansion of Chinese naval forces have raised the prospects of engagements between American and Chinese aircraft carriers if rising tension should result in open conflict.

Chinese claims to a series of islands in the South China Sea and the island state of Taiwan have prompted the US to deploy warships to demonstrate that it does not recognise Beijing's ambitions and established international freedom of navigation rules apply. The presence of US aircraft carriers to this region stretches back to the 1950s when Washington decided to include Taiwan under its

projective umbrella. Twice in the 1950s, US aircraft carriers were sent to patrol the waters between Taiwan and the Chinese mainland to deter Communist attacks. In the 1970s, the US recognised the Communist People's Republic of China (PRC) as the government of the mainland and tried to de-escalate tension by reducing US naval patrols around Taiwan. US aircraft carriers generally kept their distance except for in »

ABOVE: The USS *Carl Vinson* is home ported at San Diego and is regularly dispatched on cruises to the Western Pacific to bolster the forward deployed carrier, USS *Ronald Reagan.* (US NAVY)

BELOW: From its homeport at Yokosuka in Japan, Carrier Strike Group 5, and the USS Ronald Reagan, can rapidly respond when crisis erupt in the Western Pacific. (US NAVY)

1995 and 2005 when Washington wanted to show its displeasure at Beijing's behaviour. In 1995 the USS *Nimitz* made a transit and a decade later the USS *Kitty Hawk* sailed through the disputed straits.

After a visit to Taiwan in August 2022 by the Speaker of the US House of Representatives, Nancy Pelosi, tension escalated dramatically, and the Chinese staged a series of military exercises around the islands to demonstrate their displeasure. Further

large-scale Chinese drills took place in April 2023, involving increased flights by Chinese aircraft and live missile firings. A Chinese aircraft carrier carried out drills off Taiwan's eastern coast to demonstrate that it could be isolate the island in any conflict.

The US Navy had periodically sailed smaller warships – but not yet aircraft carriers - through the Strait of Taiwan to make the point that Washington considered them to be international waters, not Chinese territorial waters.

Since the 2022 crisis, when US warships have passed through the straits they have been provided with air cover from a US carrier, sailing nearby in the Philippine Sea.

The last major transit occurred in November 2023, involving the Arleigh Burke-class guided-missile destroyer USS *Rafael Peralta* and Royal Canadian Navy Halifax-class frigate HMCS *Ottawa* made the transit. Chinese warships and aircraft followed the progress of the two ships closely.

To provide reassurance, the US deployed two carrier strike groups, led by the USS *Ronald Reagan* and USS *Carl Vinson,* nearby. The Chinese responded putting the PLANS *Shandong,* escorted by the destroyers PLANS *Guilin* and PLANS *Changsha* and frigates PLANS *Xuchang* and PLANS *Huangshan* to sea. A few days later the PLANS *Shandong* Carrier Strike Group carried out drills with land-based combat aircraft near Taiwan. As a result, three aircraft carriers and their supporting battle groups were at sea within striking distance of Taiwan.

Chinese political leaders have ramped up their rhetoric about re-unification with Taiwan in recent years, prompting President Joe Biden to restate US commitments to defend Taiwan in time of crisis. The continued US aircraft carrier presence in the Western Pacific is meant to warn Beijing not to take a gamble that Washington would stand by if the Chinese invaded Taiwan.

BELOW: The USS *Nimitz* transits the Puget Sound en route to its homeport of Bremerton, in Washington state, in July 2023. She is the oldest aircraft carrier in US Navy service and recently got an extension to remain in frontline use. (US NAVY)

US Third Fleet

Training the Fleet

ABOVE: North Island in San Diego is the rear hub of US Pacific Fleet carrier operations and is boasts extensive facilities to repair and overhaul aircraft carriers and amphibious assault ships. Here the USS *Ronald Reagan*, USS *John C Stennis* and USS *Carl Vinson* are tied up in 2015. (US NAVY)

RIGHT: The US Pacific Fleet's aircraft carriers routinely carry out joint exercises with navies across the region. Here the Japan Maritime Self-Defense Force helicopter carrier, JS *Hyuga*, and USS *Carl Vinson* sail information during exercises close to Taiwan in response to Chinese naval deployments. (US NAVY)

From its headquarters at Naval Base Point Loma outside San Diego, in California, the US Third Fleet is responsible for naval operations along the US western seaboard, along the Alaska coast and out into the Pacific around the Hawaiian Islands.

It has the wartime mission to defend the Hawaiian Islands, Alaska and the western states of the USA but in peacetime the Third Fleet's main focus is on preparing forces forward deployment.

Five US aircraft carriers, their supporting strike groups and air wings are based in and around San Diego and Puget Sound, near Seattle, in Washington State.

The USS *Nimitz* is currently home ported at Naval Base Kitsap at Bremerton in Washington State, and part of its air wing is home based at Whidbey Island.

San Diego naval base is home port to the remaining five carriers and three of these are currently considered ready for operational tasking. The USS *Theodore Roosevelt* has been on an operational cruise in the Western Pacific since January 2024 and the other two have been operating near their home port. The USS *John C Stennis* is undergoing a refuelling and complex overhaul, or RCOH, at Norfolk in Virginia. San Diego is also home to five amphibious assault ships and their support US Marine Corps aviation units.

The main business of the Third Fleet is preparing its carriers and their supporting battle groups for operations. It has a dedicated carrier strike group staff whose sole task is to direct, execute, mentor, and assess at-sea live synthetic and academic integrated and advanced

training for warships during work up training. This training starts at the ship and air squadron level and progressively builds up into exercises for task force sized groups of ships to prepare them for working in complex operations environments.

Each year, two carrier battle groups and an amphibious ready group usually undergo pre-deployment training before heading out into the Western Pacific.

In time of major crisis or war the Third Fleet will have three main roles. It will control naval task groups protecting Hawaii, Alaska and the Western seaboard of the continental US. An important part of this homeland defence mission is to assist civil authorities after natural disasters and terrorist incidents. The fleet will also have the mission of protecting

shipping heading across the Pacific carrying supplies to keep the Seventh Fleet fighting or to reinforce the US Army in Korea.

The Third Fleet also has the mission of providing a deployable Joint Task Force headquarters, which could take command of the large naval force including at least one carrier strike group, either from a shore location or afloat. In the 1991 Gulf War, the US Navy dispatched six aircraft carriers to the Middle East and the headquarter staff of the US Seventh Fleet had to relocated to co-ordinate their operations. So, it is expected that in a major war in the Western Pacific against China or North Korea the Third Fleet would have a more forward presence to help command US Navy assets.

ABOVE: US Marine Corps F-35B Lightning IIs deployed to the Pacific region in 2021 embarked on the Royal Navy aircraft carrier, HMS *Queen Elizabeth*. (US NAVY)

BELOW: Naval Base Kitsap at Bremerton is the US Navy's second carrier home port of the Pacific seaboard and it is currently home to USS *Nimitz* and her carrier strike group. (US NAVY)

US Naval Air Force Pacific

Naval Aviation

RIGHT: The F/A-18E/F Super Hornet is the core US Pacific Fleet's carrier air wings with 17 fighter/attack squadrons operating the multi-role combat jet. (US NAVY)

US Navy aircraft carriers boast an array of state-of-the-art combat aircraft that can carry out the full spectrum of air warfare – strike, air defence, early warning, electronic warfare, anti-surface warfare and anti-submarine warfare.

To fill out the flight decks of the Pacific's fleet's seven aircraft carriers, there are six carrier air wings. There is not a one-for-one of allocation air wings for every carrier because the vessels that are out of action during maintenance do not need to have aircraft.

Each air wing is essentially an 'air force in a box' and it is designed to be able to operate as a self-contained force or be worked as part of a large joint force with other carrier air wings or with land-based air power. When not embarked on their parent carrier, naval air squadrons are home based at airfields with other squadrons that operate the same type of aircraft, working under a dedicated wing commander. This allows training and engineer support to be organised more efficiently.

US Naval Air Force Pacific not only controls the strike aircraft and helicopter wings, but it is also responsible for a number of specialist wings that provide aircraft and crews for the Atlantic coast-based carriers as well.

The Pacific Fleet is also leading the introduction of the Lockheed Martin F-35C Lightning II into the service on aircraft carrier decks. As well as leading the way with bringing US Navy F-35Cs into carrier service, US Marine Corps F-35Cs have been embarked on Pacific Fleet carriers. Four US Navy and two USMC squadrons assigned to Pacific Fleet carriers have transitioned to the F-35C.

The Boeing E/F-18E/F Super Hornets remain the core of the Pacific Fleet's fast jet aviation, with 19 squadrons operating the aircraft. Twenty squadrons fly versions

PACIFIC – CARRIER AIR WINGS, MAY 2024		
Unit	**Nickname**	**Aircraft**
All CVW staffs shore based at NAS Lemore, except for CVW 5 and CVW7		
Carrier Air Wing (CVW) 2, USS Carl Vinson		
VFA-2	Bounty Hunters	F/A-18F Super Hornet
VFA-97	Warhawks	F-35C Lightning II
VFA-113	Stingers	F/A-18E Super Hornet
VFA-192	Golden Dragons	F/A-18E Super Hornet
VAW-113	Black Eagles	E-2D Hawkeye
VAQ-136	Gauntlets	EA-18G Growler
HSC-4	Black Knights	MH-60S Seahawk
HSM-78	Blue Hawks	MH-60R Seahawk
VRM-30, Det 1	Rockhoppers	CMV-22B Osprey
Carrier Air Wing (CVW) 5, USS Ronald Reagan (MCAS Iwakuni)		
VFA-27	Royal Maces	F/A-18E Super Hornet
VFA-102	Diamondbacks	F/A-18F Super Hornet
VFA-115	Eagles	F/A-18E Super Hornet
VFA-195	Dambusters	F/A-18E Super Hornet
VAW-125	Tiger Tails	E-2D Hawkeye
VAQ-141	Shadowhawks	EA-18G Growler
HSC-12	Golden Falcons	MH-60S Seahawk
HSM-77	Saberhawks	MH-60R Seahawk
VRM-30, Det 5	Providers	CMV-22B Osprey
Carrier Air Wing (CVW) 9, USS Abraham Lincoln		
VFA-14	Tophatters	F/A-18E Super Hornet
VFA-41	Black Aces	F/A-18F Super Hornet
VFA-151	Vigilantes	F/A-18E Super Hornet
VMFA-314	Black Knights	F-35C Lightning II
VAW-117	Wallbangers	E-2D Hawkeye
VAQ-133	Wizards	EA-18G Growler
HSC-14	Chargers	MH-60S Seahawk
HSM-71	Raptors	MH-60R Seahawk
VRM-30, Det 2	Providers	CMV-22B Osprey

PACIFIC – CARRIER AIR WINGS, MAY 2024 – (CONT'D)		
Unit	Nickname	Aircraft
Carrier Air Wing (CVW) 11, USS Theodore Roosevelt		
VFA-25	Fist of the Fleet	F/A-18E Super Hornet
VFA-34	Blue Blasters	F/A-18E Super Hornet
VFA-154	Black Knights	F/A-18F Super Hornet
VFA-211	Fighting Checkmates	F/A-18E Super Hornet
VAW-115	Liberty Bells	E-2D Advanced Hawkeye
VAQ-137	Rooks	EA-18G Growler
HSC-8	Eightballers	MH-60S Seahawk
HSM-75	Wolfpack	MH-60R Seahawk
VRM-30 Det 3	Wranglers	CMV-22B Osprey
Carrier Air Wing (CVW) 17, USS Nimitz		
(curently shore based duringmaintenance period, CVW orbat from last cruise)		
VFA-22	Fighting Redcocks	F/A-18F Super Hornet
VFA-94	Shrikes	Transitioning to F/A-18E Super Hornet
VFA-137	Kestrels	F/A-18E Super Hornet
VFA-146	Blue Diamonds	F/A-18E Super Hornet
VAW-121	Sun Kings	E-2DHawkeye
VAQ-139	Cougars	EA-18G Growler
HSC-6	Indians	MH-60S Seahawk
HSM-73	Battlecats	MH-60R Seahawk
VRC-30 Det 1	Providers	C-2A Greyhound
Carrier Air Wing (CVW) 7, USS George Washington		
VFA-??		F/A-18E Super Hornet
VFA-103	Jolly Rogers	F/A-18F Super Hornet
VFA-147	Argonauts	F-35C
VFA-143	Pukin' Dogs	F/A-18E Super Hornet
VAW-121	Bluetails	E-2D Hawkeye
VAQ-140	Patriots	EA-18G Growler
HSC-5	Nightdippers	MH-60S Seahawk
HSM-46	Grandmasters	MH-60R Seahawk
VRC-40, Det 3	Amigos	C-2A Greyhound

of the Sikorsky MH-60 Seahawk maritime helicopters that embark on carriers and other warships in the Pacific region.

Electronic attack is the mission of the Boeing EA-18G Growler and all of the 15 US Navy squadrons equipped with the aircraft are based in the Pacific region, at Whidbey Island in Washington or in Japan.

Five squadrons of Northrop Grumman E-2 Hawkeye are based in California and Japan, as part of the Airborne Command, Control, Logistics Wing headquartered at Ventura County Point Mugu in California. This wing also controls all the US Navy's carrier onboard delivery (COD) units equipped with the Grumman C-2 Greyhound aircraft. A single C-2 squadron still operates in the Pacific Fleet flying supplies and personnel on and off carriers from shore bases. Fleet Logistics Multi-Mission Wing based at Naval Air Station North Island in California is bringing the Boeing CMV-22B Osprey into service into service in the COD role to eventually replace the veteran C-2. The first two squadrons CMV-22Bs are assigned to support Pacific Fleet carriers.

US Naval Air Force Pacific is also responsible for the US Navy's Boeing E-6B Mercury airborne command post and communications relay aircraft, which have the TACAMO (Take Charge And Move Out) mission to ensure communications to US naval forces around the world in the event of nuclear war.

BELOW: All US Navy 5th generation F-35C Lightning II strike squadrons are based at Naval Air Station Lemoore in California to support Pacific Fleet air wings. (US NAVY)

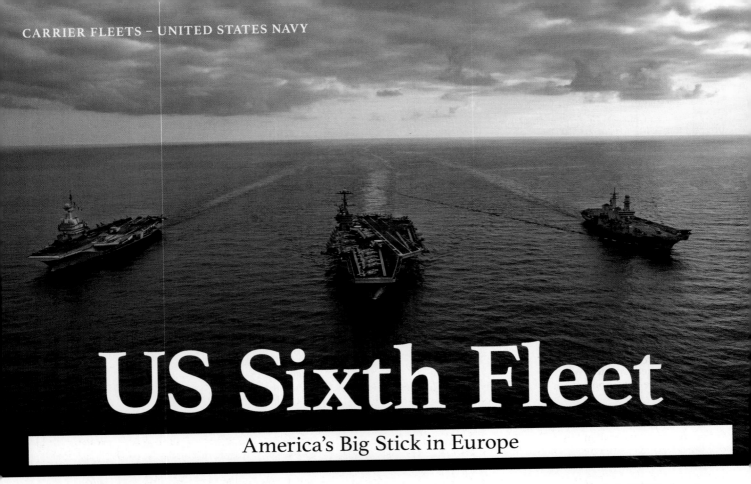

US Sixth Fleet

America's Big Stick in Europe

ABOVE: In response to the Russian invasion of Ukraine in March 2022, the FS *Charles de Gaulle*, USS *Harry S Truman* and ITS *Cavour* (left to right) gathered in the Ionian Sea to support NATO. (US NAVY)

At the height of the Cold War, the US Sixth Fleet always had an aircraft carrier battle group operating in the Mediterranean Sea. With the ending of the Balkan wars in 1999, the centre of gravity of US aircraft carrier operations shifted to the Middle East. As a result of the Ukraine War, growing tension with Russia has seen an uptick in US aircraft carrier deployments into European waters.

In the Cold War era, the Sixth Fleet dominated the Mediterranean with its aircraft carriers, and they were regularly dispatched to intervene in conflicts around the region. US carrier-borne aircraft fought dogfights with Libyan jets and bombed Lebanon in the 1980s. During the Arab Israeli wars, US aircraft carriers were also dispatched to the Eastern Mediterranean to head off Soviet intervention.

The Sixth Fleet, which was head quartered in Naples, also had an important role in NATO plans in case of war with the Soviet Union and it was envisaged that jets from its aircraft carriers would launch nuclear strikes against Soviet targets in the Black Sea region. In times of conflict, the Sixth Fleet's carriers were earmarked to be transferred to the control of NATO, as the Naval Striking and Support Forces Southern Europe (STRIKFORSOUTH). The commander of the Sixth Fleet was 'dual hatted' as head of the

RIGHT: The USS *Harry S Truman* launched around the clock air patrols over Romania and Bulgaria to bolster their air defences in the aftermath of the Russia invasion of Ukraine. (US NAVY)

STRIKFORSOUTH, because US laws prevents American nuclear weapons being controlled by non-US officers.

In a fitting finale to its Cold War role, the Sixth Fleet massed naval forces and two aircraft carriers in the Eastern Mediterranean in January 1991 to join support US air strikes against Iraq. The outbreak of conflict following the collapse of Yugoslavia in 1991, led to the United Nations and NATO intervening with peacekeeping forces. The US Navy supported these missions over the next decade by positioning an aircraft carrier in the Adriatic to launch jets to patrol no fly zones over Bosnia in 1993 and then conduct air strikes in the country in 1995. Four years later, the US carrier airpower was committed to the Kosovo conflict.

In 2004, the US military reorganised its forces in Europe and the Sixth Fleet headquarters was designated as the naval component of US European Command, or EUCOM. The fleet area of responsibility was expanded from the Mediterranean to cover all of Europe. Four years later, the Pentagon set up Africa Command, but it was not assigned its own naval component headquarters, so the Sixth Fleet was given this task. The new expanded headquarters was designated Commander, US Naval Forces Europe-Commander, US Naval Forces Africa (NAVEUR-NAVAF), with its headquarters at Capodichino outside of Naples, in the former Sixth Fleet's compound. USS *Mount Whitney*

is the Sixth Fleet flagship and is homeport nearby at Gaeta, Italy.

No US aircraft carrier is home ported in Europe, so the Sixth Fleet relies on carrier strike groups dispatched from the US Eastern seaboard. Whenever a carrier strike group enters EUCOM area of responsibility it takes on the designation Task Force 60, or TF 60. This the traditional designation of the Sixth Fleet's Battle Force, stretching back to days of the Cold War. The Sixth Fleet retains its linkages to NATO, via the Naval Striking and Support Forces NATO (STRIKFORNATO) headquarters

in Oeiras in Portugal, with the commander of the Sixth Fleet also designated to take over as STRIKFORNATO's head in time of conflict or crisis. The Sixth Fleet also regularly was assigned an amphibious ready group (ARG) with a marine expeditionary unit (MEU) embarked, to intervene in crisis situations, which is designed Task Force 61 when in European waters.

In the two decades after 2001, it was rare for Sixth Fleet to have aircraft carriers assigned for extended periods because of the demand for flat tops in the Middle East. There was a brief spike in the »

ABOVE: C-2 Greyhound carrier on-board delivery aircraft, based at the US Naval Air Station at Sigonella on Sicily, provide a logistic lifeline to US Navy aircraft carriers operating in Mediterranean region. (US NAVY)

BELOW: The US Navy's newest aircraft carrier, the USS *Gerald R Ford* made her first full length operational deployment to the Sixth Fleet from May 2023 and was away from her home port for eight months. (US NAVY)

spring of 2003, when two carriers supported the US invasion of Iraq from the Eastern Mediterranean but for the next 15 years it became very rare for the Sixth Fleet to have aircraft carriers assigned. To fill this gap, ARGs were often deployed to European waters to show the flag during major NATO exercises or in times of crisis.

In the 2011 Libyan conflict, the USS *Kearsarge* was dispatched to join the NATO air campaign. Her McDonnell Douglas AV-8B Harrier II jump jets joined the NATO air offensive, and her helicopters and marines rescued two downed US Air Force pilots from the Libyan desert.

From August to December 2016, the US conducted another operation in Libya, code-named Operation Odyssey Lightning, during the battle to capture Sirte, which was the capital of Islamic State's Libyan branch. In September 2016, the US Africa Command announced that 495 precision airstrikes were carried out by US Marine Corps AV-8B Harrier II jump jets and Bell AH-1W Cobra gunships flying from the USS *Wasp*.

The Russian occupation of Crimea in 2014 caused the US and NATO to look again at its military posture to deter future adventurism by the Kremlin. NATO looked to bolster its rapid reaction forces and the STRIKFORNATO was given an expanded role as part of the NATO Response Force, or NRF. In 2018, the new expanded NRF was put to the test in Exercise Trident Junction and USS *Harry S Truman* sailed north of the Arctic Circle in the Norwegian Sea for the first time since the collapse of the Soviet Union

During October and November 2018, STRIKFORNATO staff deployed on board USS *Mount Whitney* and performed in its role as a NATO Expanded Task Force (NETF) providing command and control of multiple strike groups. These included the USS *Iwo Jima* ARG, a Canadian/British surface action group, a Norwegian surface action group and mine countermeasures assets, a Norwegian submarine and the USS *Harry S Truman*. As a result, STRIKFORNATO commanded more than 20 ships operating in the North and Norwegian seas and troops ashore in Norway. The USS *Harry S Truman* stayed in the waters around Lofoten archipelago for the duration of the exercise.

In late 2021, as tension mounted between Russia and Ukraine, the Pentagon diverted the USS *Harry S Truman* from its planned transit through the Suez Canal to stay in the Mediterranean. US Defense Secretary Lloyd Austin wanted the US Navy to keep a consistent carrier presence in Sixth Fleet area of operations. As a result, the USS *Harry S Truman* operated in the Mediterranean Sea for eight months, making it the longest continuous operations for a US aircraft carrier in European waters in over two decades.

The carrier remained on station as Russia launched its invasion of Ukraine at the end of February 2022 and was soon tasked to launch its fighters to join NATO combat air patrols over the Black Sea region. US Air Force and British tanker aircraft provided air-to-air refuelling

LEFT: The USS *Harry S Truman* (rear) and USS *Theodore Roosevelt* (front) sailed to European waters in 2014 as a show of force after the Crimea crisis with Russia. (US NAVY)

support for the long missions up over Greece and Bulgaria. At times during the deployment, Carrier Air Wing 1 launched 80 to 90 sorties a day from the USS *Harry S Truman's* deck to support NATO. In late February 2022, a detachment of the carrier's Boeing F/A-18E/F Super Hornets and Boeing EA-18 Growlers spent a week operating from Fetesti Airbase, in Romania, carrying out air policing sorties, supported by the USAF's 435th Air Ground Operations Wing and the 606th Air Control Squadron.

After nine months away from home, the carrier returned home to Naval Station Norfolk in Virginia on September 12, 2022. The ship sailed more than 65,000 nautical miles, all while conducting multiple operations in the region to include enhanced air policing missions, dual and tri-carrier operations, and the NATO-led-vigilance activities Neptune Shield 22 and Neptune Strike 22. During its historic deployment, the carrier strengthened relationships with NATO Allies and partners.

"The Truman and our embarked air wing were the central pillar of the strike group," said Rear Admiral Paul Spedero, commander of the USS *Harry S Truman* Strike Group. "The carrier isn't just a weapon of war, it is a symbol of American commitment and attention – one that has been focused on reassuring our NATO Allies and other European partners of our commitment to peace, stability, and cooperation."

Continuing tension with Russia meant that the USS *Harry S Truman* was relieved in the Mediterranean by USS *George HW Bush* for the next seven months. The carriers briefly operated together in the Mediterranean, marking the first time two aircraft carriers had been in the region for 19 years. »

BELOW: F/A-18E Super Hornets operating from US aircraft carriers in European waters routinely integrate with NATO air forces for training exercises. (US NAVY)

In the autumn of 2022, the US Navy's newest carrier, the USS *Gerald R Ford* forayed into Europe waters for several weeks to join exercises with allied navies in the Eastern Atlantic

The following May, USS *Gerald R Ford* departed Naval Station Norfolk on her first full length deployment and worked in the Sixth Fleet's Area of Responsibility (AOR). At the end of May 2023, she made a port visit to the Norwegian capital, Oslo, before joint naval exercises in Norwegian waters. In June 2023, she sailed into the Mediterranean for exercises with the Italian navy.

On October 8, 2023, the day after the Hamas attack on Israel, the USS *Gerald R Ford* carrier strike group was ordered to sail at speed to the Eastern Mediterranean "to bolster regional deterrence efforts." Along with the cruiser USS *Normandy*, and the destroyers USS *Ramage*, USS *Carney*, USS *Roosevelt* and USS *Thomas Hudner*. The US further bolstered its naval presence in the Middle East when the USS *Dwight D. Eisenhower* and Carrier Strike Group 2 arrived in the Mediterranean, en route to Red Sea and Indian Ocean.

In December 2023, the USS *Gerald R Ford* was relieved in the Mediterranean Sea by the USS *Bataan* Amphibious Ready Group and set sail for its home port of Norfolk, Virginia.

Atlantic Coast Carriers

United States Fleet Forces Command

The US Atlantic Fleet was first formed in 1906 and it played an important role in World War Two and then the Cold War. The historic title was lost in 2006 when it was renamed United States Fleet Forces Command, or USFF, to better reflect its force generation role.

After the ending of the Cold War in 1990, and the demise of the Soviet naval threat, US Navy aircraft carriers lost their operation role in the North Atlantic.

East coast-based carriers were concentrated at Naval Station Norfolk in Virginia, in between operational cruises to Europe and the Middle East. Carrier strike groups undergo intense work up training to prepare them for their work in operational theatre.

Aircraft carriers based at Norfolk were scrambled to help protect American cities in the few weeks after the 9/11 attacks in New York and Washington DC in September 2001.

Norfolk is now the focus of US aircraft carrier operations the Atlantic, European and Middle Eastern waters. Four carriers, the USS *Dwight D Eisenhower*, USS *Harry S Truman*, USS *George HW Bush* and USS *Gerald R Ford*, are now operating from Naval Station Norfolk. Pacific Fleet carriers, the USS *George Washington* and USS *John C Stennis* have temporarily relocated to the Newport News shipyard across Hampton Roads from Naval Station Norfolk while they undergo major overhauls.

USFF has its headquarters in the Naval Support Activity Hampton Roads in Norfolk, Virginia, and has an emergency role to support US Northern Command during major homeland security incidents.

US Southern Command is responsible for US military operations in the Caribbean and South America. Its naval component is the Fourth Fleet, based at Naval Station Mayport in Florida. The fleet rarely has aircraft carriers assigned to it, but it is common for them to undertake work up cruises in the region after they have completed major overhauls at Newport News.

BELOW LEFT: The aircraft carriers USS *Dwight D Eisenhower*, USS *George HW Bush*, USS *Enterprise*, USS *Harry S Truman*, and USS *Abraham Lincoln* in port at Naval Station Norfolk in 2012. It is the world's largest naval base. (US NAVY)

BELOW RIGHT: Norfolk has a long association with carrier aviation. The US Navy's first aircraft carrier, the USS *Langley*, which had the pennant CV-1, was convert into a flat top in Norfolk naval yard in 2021. (US NAVY)

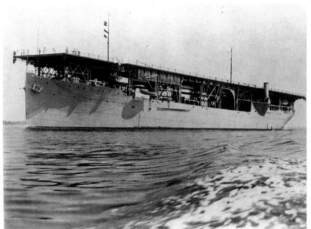

US CARRIER STRIKE GROUPS – ATLANTIC, MAY 2024				
Carrier Strike Group (CSG)	**CSG-8**	**CSG-2**	**CSG-10**	**CSG-12**
Location	Mid Atlantic	Mediterranean	Norfolk, VA	Norfolk, VA
Aircraft Carrier (CVN)	USS Harry S Truman (CVN 75)	USS Dwight D. Eisenhower (CVN 69)	USS George HW Bush (CVN 77)	USS Gerald R Ford (CVN 78)
Carrier Air Group (CVW)	*CVW 1*	*CVW 3*	*CVW-7*	*CVW 8*
Ticonderoga-class cruisers	USS San Jacinto (CG-56)	USS Philippine Sea (CG-58)	USS Leyte Gulf (CG-55)	USS Normandy (CG-60)
Destroyer Squadron	*DESRON-28*	*DESRON-22*	*DESRON-26*	*DESRON-2*
Arleigh Burke-class destroyerd	USS Bainbridge (DDG-96)	USS Gravely (DDG-107)	USS Delbert D. Black (DDG-119)	USS Ramage (DDG 61)
	USS Cole (DDG-67)	USS Mason (DDG-87)	USS Truxtun (DDG-103)	USS McFaul (DDG 74)
	USS Gravely (DDG-107)	USS *Laboon* (DDG-58)	USS Farragut (DDG-99)	USS Thomas Hudner (DDG 116)
	USS Jason Dunham (DDG-109)			
Date of Deployment and CSG composition	Apr-24	Apr-24	Aug-22	Oct-23

US Second Fleet

Keeping the Sea Lanes Open

ALARM

ABOVE: Newport News shipyard in Norfolk is the only site where US Navy nuclear aircraft carriers can have their nuclear reactors refuelled. (US NAVY)

BELOW: The USS *Dwight D Eisenhower* is a work horse of Norfolk-based aircraft carriers and during the winter of 2023 and 2024 she saw action in the Red Sea. (US NAVY)

In 2018, the US Navy re-established its Second Fleet at Naval Station Norfolk in Virginia to be responsible for naval operations across most of the western North Atlantic.

Its area of responsibility includes some 6,700,000 square miles of the Atlantic Ocean from the North Pole to the Caribbean and from the shores of the United States to the middle of the Atlantic Ocean.

It was given the mission to defend the maritime avenues of approach between North America and Europe, to ensure the lines of communications between the two continents in time of conflict.

The commander of the Second Fleet is dual-hatted as the commander of NATO's Joint Force Command Norfolk, which reports to the Supreme Allied Commander Europe. This is to ensure that in time of conflict or major crisis US naval power in the Atlantic will be seamlessly integrated to NATO war plans. Under these plans the Second Fleet would come under command of NATO headquarters in Europe to allow an integrated naval campaign to be waged in the North Atlantic and Arctic regions.

Since 2018, the Second Fleet has been developing plans to use its naval assets, including its aircraft carrier battle groups, to counter Russian naval forces in the North Atlantic.

Russian warships and submarines armed with long range cruise and hypersonic missile are making forays out into the North Atlantic so NATO navies have had to plan to neutralise these forces it war should break out. In peacetime, the Second Fleet is closely involved in NATO efforts to track Russian submarines and surface vessels on a 24/7/365 basis.

Within the US Navy chain of command, the Second Fleet reports to the headquarters of US Fleet Forces (USFF) for homeland security operations and other mission that might be required by the US government.

The Second Fleet controls the four aircraft carriers based at Naval Station Norfolk when they are held ready for short notice deployments to Europe or the Middle East.

Four carrier strike group (CSG) and Expeditionary Strike Group (ESG) staffs are assigned to the Second Fleet, and they are permanent headquarters organisations that control active aircraft carriers, their air wing and supporting warships for extended periods. They normally embark on a flag ship or can also establish headquarters from shore locations.

The Second Fleet's role in projecting naval power into the North Atlantic to keep open lines of communication to Europe was put to the test between January and March 2024 during NATO's Exercise Steadfast Defender.

A 100-strong command team from the Second Fleet and ESG 2 deployed to the Norwegian airfield at Bodø, to establish a maritime command element, Commander Task Force North (CTF-N). The Whidbey Island-class dock landing ship USS Gunston Hall sailed to Norway to act as CTF-N's command ship. During the exercise, the British strike carrier HMS Prince of Wales and the Italian carrier, ITS Giuseppe Garibaldi, worked together in CTF-N. The task force sailed off the far north of Norway, practiced carrying out anti-submarine operations, landed an amphibious force on the Norwegian coast and launched simulated strike missions against land targets.

ABOVE: Newport News shipyard in Norfolk is the only site where US Navy nuclear aircraft carriers can have their nuclear reactors refuelled. (US NAVY)

BELOW: The USS John C Stennis is currently undergoing a major overhaul and refuel at Newport News Shipyard. (US NAVY)

Wings of the Atlantic Fleet

Naval Aviation

ABOVE: Oceana Naval Air Station is home to Atlantic coast-based carrier air wings and their F/A-18E/F Super Hornet squadrons. (US NAVY)

US Navy aircraft carriers boast an array of state-of-the-art combat aircraft that can carry out the full spectrum of air warfare – strike, air defence, early warning, electronic warfare, anti-surface warfare and anti-submarine warfare.

To fill out the flights decks of the four aircraft carriers based on the Atlantic coast, there are four carrier air wings (CVW).

Each air wing is essentially an 'air force in a box' and it is designed to be able operate as a self-contained force or be work as part of a large joint force with other carrier air wings or with land-based air power. When not embarked on their parent carrier, naval air squadrons are home based at airfields with other squadrons that operate the same type of aircraft, working under a dedicated wing commander. This allows training

and engineer support to organised more efficiently.

Naval Air Force Atlantic has one strike fighter wing and two helicopter wings to control its squadrons when they are ashore at their home bases. Specialist airborne early warning and carrier on-board deliver squadrons are based on the eastern seaboard are under the command of Pacific coast wings. All electronic warfare squadrons are based at Whidbey

Island and dispatch aircraft and crews to Atlantic-coast based carriers.

The Commander of the Naval Air Force Atlantic reports to the headquarters US Fleet Forces (USFF) Command and it is responsible for training and preparing naval air squadrons for operational duty on aircraft carrier.

The Boeing E/F-18E/F Super Hornets remain the core of the Atlantic coast aviation, with 15 squadrons operating the aircraft. Eighteen squadrons fly versions of the Sikorsky MH-60 Seahawk maritime helicopters that embark on carriers and other warships in the Atlantic region.

The US Navy eventually plans to buy 260 5th generation Lockheed Martin F-35C Lightning II, but the stealth jet has yet to enter service on an Atlantic-based aircraft carriers. It is expected the USS *George HW Bush* will embark the jets for the first time on an operational cruise in 2025.

Four squadrons of Northrop Grumman E-2 Hawkeye and Grumman C-2 Greyhound squadron are based at Naval Station Norfolk, as part of the Airborne Command, Control, Logistics Wing. The Boeing CMV-22B Osprey is coming service into service in the carrier-on-board delivery (COD) role to eventually replace the veteran C-2 but an squadron is not yet equipped with this new aircraft to support Atlantic-based carriers.

The US Navy's airborne mine-counter measures force, which operates three squadrons equipped with the Sikorsky MH-53E Sea Dragon helicopters, is also based at Naval Station Norfolk.

ATLANTIC – CARRIER AIR WINGS, MAY 2024		
Unit	**Nickname**	**Aircraft**
All CVW staffs shore based at NAS Oceana		
Carrier Air Wing (CVW) 1, USS Harry S. Truman		
VFA-11	Red Rippers	F/A-18F Super Hornet
VFA-81	Sunliners	F/A-18E Super Hornet
VFA-136	KnightHawks	F/A-18E Super Hornet
VFA-143	Pukin Dogs	F/A-18E Super Hornet
VAW-126	Seahawks	F/A-18G Growler
VAQ-144	Main Battery	E-2D Hawkeye
HSC-11	Dragon Slayers	SH-60R Sea Hawk
HSM-72	Proud Warriors	C-2 Greyhound
VRC-40, Det 1	Hustlers	SH-60S Sea Hawk
Carrier Air Wing (CVW) 3, USS Dwight D. Eisenhower		
VFA-32	Swordsmen	F/A-18F Super Hornet
VFA-83	Rampagers	F/A-18E Super Hornet
VFA-105	Gunslingers	F/A-18E Super Hornet
VFA-131	Wildcats	F/A-18E Super Hornet
VAW-123	Screwtops	E-2C Hawkeye
VAQ-130	Zappers	EA-18G Growler
HSC-7	Dusty Dogs	MH-60S Seahawk
HSM-74	Swamp Foxes	MH-60R Seahaw
VRC-40, Det 4	Mambas	C-2A Greyhound
Carrier Air Wing (CVW) 8, USS Gerald R. Ford		
VFA-31	Tomcatters	F/A-18E Super Hornet
VFA-37	Ragin Bulls	F/A-18E Super Hornet
VFA-87	Golden Warriors	F/A-18E Super Hornet
VFA-213	Black Lions	F/A-18F Super Hornet
VAW-124	Bear Aces	E-2D Hawkeye
VAQ-142	Gray Wolves	EA-18G Growler
HSC-9	Tridents	MH-60S Seahawk
HSM-70	Spartans	MH-60R Seahawk
VRC-40, Det 2	Deuce/Bushwackers	C-2A Greyhound

BELOW: The first CMV-22B Osprey tilt rotor arrived at Norfolk Naval Station in April 2024 to allow Fleet Logistics Multi-Mission Squadron (VRM) 40 to begin converting to its new aircraft. (US NAVY)

In the Sandbox

US Aircraft Carriers in the Middle East

RIGHT: The 1991 Gulf War eventually saw six US aircraft carriers massed in the Middle East. This saw the Forrestal-class aircraft carrier, USS *Saratoga,* join the air offensive against Iraq and one of its Vietnam-war era A-6E Intruders was shot down. (US NAVY)

BELOW: The USS *Dwight D Eisenhower* in the 'big ditch' - as US sailors call the Suez Canal – in August 1990 after being mobilised to sail to the Middle East in response to Iraqi invasion of Kuwait. (US NAVY)

In August 1990, Iraqi troops invaded Kuwait and set in motion a series of events that culminated in 500,000 US troops massing in the Middle East for Operation Desert Storm. The coalition offensive to retake Kuwait began on January 17, 1991, and was the largest air operation since World War Two. US Navy aircraft from six aircraft carriers sailing in the Arabian Gulf and Red Sea with more than 400 aircraft embarked played a leading role in the ten-week long war.

This was the start of more than three decades of almost continuous US carrier presence in Middle East waters, launching aircraft into action over Iraq, Afghanistan, Syria and Yemen. Today, the US Navy's Fifth Fleet is the naval component of US

Central Command and controls US and coalition naval operations in the Arabian Gulf, Indian Ocean and Red Sea regions. Back in 1990, there was

no dedicated fleet-level command in the Middle East, so the Seventh Fleet headquarters temporarily re-located to the region to take control of US

ABOVE: Ten ships of Task Force 155 gather in the Red Sea during Operation Desert Storm in February 1991, including the USS *Saratoga*, USS *America* and USS *John F Kennedy*. (US NAVY)

naval forces operating against Iraq during Operations Desert Shield and then Desert Storm.

US military planners devised a massive air campaign to neutralise Iraq's air force and long-range missile capability, ahead of a land invasion by coalition troops to liberate Kuwait. The US Navy massed six aircraft carriers to join this offensive. Battle Force Yankee or Task Force 155, operated in the Red Sea and Task Force 154, or Battle Force Zulu, massed in the Arabian Sea and Gulf. For the duration of Operation Desert Storm, the carriers launched hundreds of sorties a day into the skies over Iraq and Kuwait. At first, they blitzed strategic targets, such as airfields, Scud missile launchers and supply dumps, before switching to flying close air support for advancing coalition grounds troops. This was a classic strike carrier role.

Once the Iraqis retreated from Kuwait and signed a ceasefire agreement, the bulk of US forces were withdrawn from the Middle East, but a residual force remained to police a series of no-fly zones set up over Iraq to limit the country's ability to threaten its neighbours. For a decade, the US Navy dispatched carriers into the Arabian Gulf to contribute to the no-fly zone enforcement missions. They launched daily patrols to ensure Iraqi aircraft remained on the ground and regularly bombed Iraqi surface-to-air missile launchers that opened fire on coalition aircraft.

In 1995, the US Navy upgraded its naval command in the Middle East by re-establishing the Fifth Fleet, with its headquarters on the island of »

LEFT: The classic F-14 Tomcat saw service in both the 1991 and 2003 wars against Iraq, before being retired from service in 2006.

Bahrain, as the naval component of US Central Command or NAVCENT. US Navy aircraft carriers and supporting warships continued to rotate into the Middle East for six month-long deployments from the Pacific and Atlantic Fleets.

The 9/11 attacks on New York and Washington DC set in motion two decades of continuous US combat operations in Afghanistan, Iraq and Syria under the banner of the Global War on Terror. US troops moved into the Middle East and required constant air support. The 2003 invasion of Iraq saw four aircraft carriers massed in the Arabian Gulf, with their 408 aircraft flying 8,945 sorties during the three week-long war.

Throughout operations in the Middle East since 1991, US Navy aircraft carriers have worked in close co-operation with the US Air Force. All US and coalition air operations were co-ordinated from a centralised Combined Air Operation Centre or CAOC, which generated a daily air tasking order, or ATO, assigning missions to individual aircraft and squadrons. US Navy carrier-borne aircraft operated within the ATO system and each carrier air wing dispatched air liaison officers to the CAOC to help generate each day's ATO.

The huge distances involved in providing air support for US troops inside Iraq and Afghanistan meant US Navy pilots had to rely heavily on the US Air Force or coalition air-to-air refuelling tankers. They allowed US Navy jets to remain on station for extended periods, without having to return to their carriers to refuel.

As America's wars in the Middle East and Afghanistan ebbed and flowed after 2001, carriers would be surged into the region when they were needed. From 2010 through 2013, the US Navy tried to maintain two aircraft carriers east of Suez, known as a '2.0 carrier presence,' although it sometimes temporarily dipped below that level. The heightened presence aimed to provide air and sea striking power for US operations in Iraq and Afghanistan, and also to deter Iran from bad behaviour in the region and keep the Strait of Hormuz open.

RIGHT: US Marine Corps AV-8B Harrier II jump jets received their combat debut in the 1991 Gulf War, including flying from shore bases and a so-called 'Harrier Carriers' sailing in the waters of the Northern Arabian Gulf. (US NAVY)

BELOW: After 1990 the USS *Dwight D Eisenhower* was a regular visitor to the Middle East, including in 2013, as seen here passing through the Suez Canal. (US NAVY)

Although land-based US Air Force aircraft could have in theory have conducted almost all US air support missions in the Middle East from 2001 onwards the Pentagon liked to keep aircraft carriers on hand in case political objections from region allies interrupted land-based operations. Arab countries routinely imposed restrictions on the type of missions that could be flown from air bases in their countries or closed off air space. US Navy aircraft carrier flight decks counted as sovereign US territory and did not require host nation approval for missions to be flown.

The Fifth Fleet's main carrier battle force is known as Task Force 50 and whenever a carrier strike group enters the NAVCENT area of responsibility, it adopts that designation. US amphibious ready groups when operating under

NAVCENT adopt the designation Task Force 51.

US carrier operations in the Middle East peaked again between 2014 and early 2019, as the war against Islamic State in Iraq and Syria escalated. US Navy jets flew in the first strike missions against Islamic State fighters advancing into Iraq in August 2014 by McDonnell Douglas F/A-18 Hornets from the USS *George HW Bush*.

The defeat of the last Islamic State enclave in Syria in the spring of 2019 led to a reduction of US air operations across the Middle East and for months at a time there was no need for a US aircraft carrier or amphibious ready group in the region. Growing tension with Russia and China led the US Navy to prioritise these theatres of operation over the Middle East. In March 2021, the French aircraft carrier FS *Charles de Gaulle* filled this

gap and assumed the command of Task Force 50 for several weeks.

USS *Ronald Reagan* was on station in the Arabian Sea in the summer of 2021, along with the USS *Iowa Jima* Amphibious Ready Group, to provide support for the final withdrawal of US troops from Afghanistan. Jets from the USS *Ronald Reagan* flew air patrols over Kabul airport as US troops protected the loading of more than 150,000 civilians onto evacuation flights but were not called into action before the last US soldiers left Afghanistan on August 30.

Task Force 50 was reactivated in November 2023 with the arrival in the Red Sea of the USS *Dwight D Eisenhower* in response to attacks on civilian shipping by Houthi rebels in Yemen. The carrier and her strike group remained under the command of NAVCENT until April 2024 when they moved into the Mediterranean.

ABOVE LEFT: Four US aircraft carriers were massed for the 2003 Iraq war, including the USS *Harry S Truman*, and their embarked aircraft flew 8,945 sorties during the three week-long war. (US NAVY)

ABOVE RIGHT: Operation Desert Storm in 1991 was the start of more than 30 years of US military engagement in the Middle East that required the near continuous presence of US Navy aircraft carriers or amphibious assault ships in the region. (US NAVY)

Lightning Carriers

Amphibious Ready Groups

The US Navy operates a fleet of nine amphibious assault ships that are capable of operating up to a dozen fast jets in support for US Marine Corps operations.

These vessels are bigger than the aircraft carriers operated by many other navies, and they are increasingly being used by the US Navy to fill gaps in the deployment schedule of their 100,000-ton Nimitz-class aircraft carriers.

By the end of 2025, the US Marine Corps hopes to have retired the last of its McDonnell Douglas AV-8B Harrier II jump jets in favour of the 5th generation Lockheed Martin F-35B Lightning II stealth combat aircraft. The potential of these new jets to transform US Navy power projection operations has resulted in the amphibious assault ships being nicknamed 'Lightning Carriers'.

The Wasp- and America-class vessels are designed to be flagships of Amphibious Ready Groups (ARGs) that deliver a 2,200 strong Marine Expeditionary Unit (MEU) onto hostile shorelines by landing craft, hovercraft or helicopters. Each MEU has an aviation element that combines AV-8Bs or F-35B, Boeing MV-22 Osprey tilt rotors, Bell AH-1Z Cobra gunships, Sikorsky CH-53E heavy lift helicopters and Bell UH-1Y Huey utility helicopters.

When embarked on an ARG, a MEU is intended to be a '9/11 emergency force' that quickly moves to a crisis zone to carry out non-combat evacuation operations (NEO), humanitarian missions or small-scale combat tasks. By providing it with a mix of aviation, landing craft, hovercraft and ground combat personnel, a MEU is self-contained and be deployed quickly without having to wait for reinforcements or specialist capabilities.

The US amphibious assault ships have large flat top-flight decks to allow fixed wing or helicopter operations. Both the

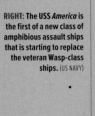

RIGHT: The USS *America* is the first of a new class of amphibious assault ships that is starting to replace the veteran Wasp-class ships. (US NAVY)

BELOW: The F-35B Lightning II 5th generation combat aircraft is now embarked on all Pacific Fleet amphibious assault ships and is soon to replace the AV-8B Harrier II in Atlantic coast -based amphibious ready groups. (US NAVY)

AV-8B and F-35B have vertical take-off and landing (VTOL) capabilities so do not require catapults or arrester wires.

A MEU usually embarked a contingent of six AV-8Bs or F-35Bs, but the US amphibious ships have the space to embark up to 20 jump jets if needed. In the 2003 invasion of Iraq, USS *Bataan* and USS *Bonhomme Richard*, operated a so-called 'Harrier Carriers' with their flights decks full of AV-8Bs to support their marine units that had moved ashore.

The growth of range and capabilities of Chinese anti-ship missiles has prompted renewed interest in increasing the use of the assault ships as 'Lightning Carriers'. The 100,000-ton Nimitz-class carriers are being seen as too vulnerable and valuable to risk moving them into the engagement rings of Chinese anti-ship missiles. The smaller assault ships are considered more expendable, so the US Navy and Marine Corps is looking to push them further forward towards Chinese defences. When loaded with up to a 20 F-35Bs, these Lightning Carriers will still pack a useful punch, but their small size, manoeuvrability and small radar cross section will make them more survivable in high threat zones around the South China Sea.

The Wasp-class assault ships were first ordered in the 1980s and they are starting to show their age. In early 2024, seven of the nine assaults ships were undergoing maintenance or working up after being out of action. This has led to several gaps when ARGs were not available in the Middle East or European waters. Two new America-class vessels are being built and funding has been found for a fifth, but the Pentagon has not committed to replacing all the Wasp-class with new ships as they reach the end of the operational lives.

ABOVE: San Diego is the home port of the Pacific Fleet's amphibious assault vessels. (US NAVY)

BELOW: US Marine Expeditionary Units routinely stage exercises with allies in the Pacific region to bolster links with America's allies. (US NAVY)

US AMPHIBIOUS READY GROUPS, MAY 2024				
Amphibious Ready Group (ARG)	**America ARG**	**Boxer ARG**	**Bataan ARG**	**Wasp ARG**
Location	South China Sea	San Diego/South China Sea	Norfolk	Eastern Altantic
Landing Helicopter Assault (LHA)	USS America (LHA-6)			
Landing Helicopter Dock (LHD)		USS Boxer (LHD-4)	USS Bataan (LHD-5	USS Wasp (USS Wasp)
Landing Platform Dock (LPD)	USS San Diego (LPD 22)	USS Somerset (LPD-25)	USS Mesa Verde (LPD 19)	USS New York (LPD 21)
Landing Ship Dock (LSD)	USS Pearl Harbor (LSD 52)	USS Harpers Ferry (LSD-49)	USS Carter Hall (LSD 50)	USS Oak Hill (LSD 51)
Marine Expeditionary Unit (MEU)	*31st MEU*	*15th MEU*	*26th MEU*	*24th MEU*
Battalion Landing Team	1/1 Marines	1/5 Marines	1/6 Marines	1/8 Marines
Marine Medium Tiltrotor Squadron (Reinforced) (VMM)	*VMM-265(Rein)*	*VMM-165 (Rein)*	*VMM-162 (Rein)*	*VMM-365 (Rein)*
Tilt Rotor (MV-22B)	12	12	12	12
Heavy Lift Helicopters (CH-53E)	4	4	4	4
Attach Helicopters (AH-1Z)	4	4	4	4
Utility Helicopters (UH-1Y)	3	3	3	3
Marine Fighter Attack/Attack Squadron (VMFA/VMA)	*VMFA-121*	*VMFA-225*	*VMA-231*	*VMA-223*
Attack Jets	6 x F-35B	6 x F-35B	6 x AV-8B	6 x AV-8B

Gator Navy

US Marine Corps Aviation

ABOVE: 5th generation F-35B Lightning IIs are transforming the combat capabilities of US Marine Expeditionary Units. (US NAVY)

Expeditionary operations are at the heart of US Marine Corps (USMC) air support doctrine. Its McDonnell Douglas AV-8B Harrier II jump jets will be replaced in favour of the 5th generation Lockheed Martin F-35B Lightning II stealth combat aircraft. These jets are designed to be able to operate from small assault ships or to fly from austere landing strips ashore.

RIGHT: VM-22B Osprey tilt-rotors carry US Marines ashore during air operations from US Navy amphibious assault ships. (US NAVY)

Wherever in the world US Marines have to fight, they are guaranteed to have USMC jet flying overhead to deliver close air support against enemy positions. In World War Two, Korea and Vietnam, USMC fighter attack squadrons operated from airstrips on the edge of the battlefield. The arrival of the first Harriers in the 1970s removed the USMC reliance of runways. Its AV-8As and Bs could fly ashore from assault ships and operate

alongside helicopters. The F-35B was specifically designed to take the place of the Harrier but added stealth or low observable features to neutralise enemy radars.

The last two Harrier attack (VMA) squadrons are due to transition to the F-35B by 2026/27 and they continue to fly from Atlantic coast-based amphibious ships. All the West coast and Japanese-based VMA squadrons that fly the F-35B. VMA-223 and VMA-231 remain as the last USMC operators of the AV-8B.

The USMC currently augments its Harriers and F-35Bs with McDonnell Douglas F/A-18C/D Hornets to fly offensive strike missions deep behind enemy lines or flight combat air patrols to protect bridgeheads from enemy aircraft. It is intended that all the Hornets will be replaced by Lightnings.

The USMC is procuring 353 F-35B and 67 F-35C, a total of 420 aircraft at the rate of roughly 20 aircraft per year. After completing the F-35 transition, 18 active-component F-35 operational squadrons will enable the

Squadron Name	Aircraft	Transition (Year)	Nickname	Senior Command	Station
US MARINE CORPS – ATTACK/FIGHTER ATTACK SQUADRONS, MAY 2024					
VMA-223	AV-8B	F-35B (2026)	Bulldogs	MAG-14, 2nd MAW	MCAS Cherry Point, NC
VMA-231	AV-8B	F-35B (2027)	Ace of Spades	MAG-14, 2nd MAW	MCAS Cherry Point, NC
VMFA-112	F/A-18C	F-35B (2030)	Cowboys	MAG-41, 4th MAW	NASJRB Fort Worth, TX
VMFA-115	Nil	F-35C (2027)	Silver Eagles	MAG-14, 2nd MAW	MCAS Cherry Point, NC
VMFA-134	Nil	F-35B (2030)	Smoke	MAG-11, 3rd MAW	MCAS Miramar, CA
VMFA-121	F-35B		Green Knights	MAG-12, 1st MAW	MCAS Iwakuni, Japan
VMFA-122	F-35B		Flying Leathernecks	MAG-13, 3rd MAW	MCAS Yuma, AZ
VMFA-211	F-35B		Wake Island Avengers	MAG-13, 3rd MAW	MCAS Yuma, AZ
VMFA-214	F-35B		Black Sheep	MAG-13, 3rd MAW	MCAS Yuma, AZ
VMFA(AW)-224	F/A-18D	F-35B (2026)	Bengals	MAG-31, 2nd MAW	MCAS Beaufort, SC
VMFA-225	F-35B		Vikings	MAG-13, 3rd MAW	MCAS Yuma, AZ
VMFA-232	F/A-18C	F-35B (2030)	Red Devils	MAG-11, 3rd MAW	MCAS Miramar, CA
VMFA-242	F-35B		Bats	MAG-12, 1st MAW	MCAS Iwakuni, Japan
VMFA-251	Nil	F-35C (2025)	Thuderbolts	MAG-14, 2nd MAW	MCAS Cherry Point, NC
VMFA-311	F-35C		Tomcats	MAG-11, 3rd MAW	MCAS Miramar, CA
VMFA-312	F/A-18C	F-35B (2028)	Checkerboard	MAG-31, 2nd MAW	MCAS Beaufort, SC
VMFA-314	F-35C		Black Knights	MAG-11, 3rd MAW	MCAS Miramar, CA
VMFA-323	F/A-18C	F-35B (2029)	Death Rattlers	MAG-11, 3rd MAW	MCAS Miramar, CA
VMFA-533	F-35B		Hawks	MAG-31, 2nd MAW	MCAS Beaufort, SC
VMFA-542	F-35B		Tigers	MAG-14, 2nd MAW	MCAS Cherry Point, NC
Training Units					
VMFAT-501	F-35B		Warlords	MAG-31, 2nd MAW	MCAS Beaufort, SC
VMFAT-502	F-35B		Flying Nighmares	MAG-11, 3rd MAW	MAG-31, 2nd MAW
Test and Evaluation Units					
VMX-1	various		Flying Lions	OT&E Force	MCAS Yuma, AZ

Notes

VMA: Marine Attack Squadron; VFMA: Marine Fighter Attack Squadron; VFMA(AW): Marine Fighter Attack Squadron (All Weather); VMFAT: Marine Fighter Attack Training Squadrons; VMX: Marine Operational Test and Evaluation Squadron; MAG: Marine Air Group; MAW: Marine Air Wing; MCAS: Marine Corps Air Station

Marine Corps to meet its operational requirements.

USMC fixed wing squadrons have long embarked on US Navy aircraft carriers as part of their air wings. This is intended to make the USMC's expertise in close air support available to carrier air wings. Today this is dubbed Tactical Air Integration (TAI) and as a result USMC Hornet squadrons routinely embark on aircraft carriers for six-month long deployments as part of US Navy air wings. To continue to meet its TAI commitments, the USMC is planning to field four squadrons of F-35C, which are 'cats and traps' compatible. This variant of the Lightning has a bigger wing for improved carrier landing performance and gives it extended range.

In January 2022, VMFA-314 departed Naval Base San Diego onboard the USS *Abraham Lincoln*, making it the first USMC F-35C squadron to deploy on an aircraft carrier. Three more USMC Hornet squadrons are to convert to the F-35C by 2028.

Carrier Future

Flat Tops in the 21st Century

RIGHT: Laser weapons, such as Britain's Dragon Fire, are soon to be installed on navy warships to replace surface-to-air missiles.
(MOD/CROWN COPYRIGHT)

More than 100 years since the first aircraft landed on a ship, naval airpower has come on in leaps and bounds. Today there are 35 flat top carriers in service with 10 navies and seven more carriers are under construction, with seven more planned.

Many critics have claimed the day of the aircraft carrier is over – they are too expensive, too vulnerable to modern weapons and drones are making them redundant. Yet in the last 15 years, the Chinese navy has joined the world carrier operators list with gusto, putting three big 'flat top' carriers, equipped with a fleet of modern high performance fighter jets, to sea. Britain rejoined the carrier club after a seven year long break and Japan is getting back into the carrier game for the first time since World War Two.

In a sign that nothing stands still in the world of naval technology, Turkey is on the verge of putting a carrier too sea that operates unmanned drones as its main fixed wing offensive aircraft.

Navies around the world see the value of flat tops as the core of naval

BELOW: Unmanned aircraft or drones are now regularly flying from aircraft carriers as navies experiment with these revolutionary weapons.
(US NAVY)

task groups, providing air defence, strike capabilities against land targets and contributing to the defence against submarines. Although the types of aircraft operated from carriers is beyond recognition compared to biplanes of 100 years ago, the role and missions they fly are essentially the same. Only by securing the skies above their fleets can they be protected from attack.

Flat tops are essentially floating airfields that can be manoeuvred to within range of enemy territory from unexpected directions and then withdraw to a safe distance after hitting the enemy hard. This strike role was proved by the British at Taranto in 1940 and then a year later by the Japanese at Pearl Harbor. This concept remains valid today, even if

precision guided weapons and stealth aircraft are now the main strike weapons of naval aviation.

Growing tensions in the Indo-Pacific region has seen aircraft carriers return to centre stage as the core of naval battlegroups, potentially looking to strike at enemy's carriers to secure naval dominance. The confrontation of Taiwan has seen US and Chinese carrier battlegroups manoeuvre for advantage. In the future Japanese, British and possibly Indian aircraft carriers could join this duel.

The advantages of carrier airpower are prompting America, France and China to look to build new nuclear-powered 'super' carriers to keep them in carrier game for the rest of the century. Britain has just brought two 65,000-ton carriers into service and its expecting to be in service for another 50 years. India and China are already looking to add new carriers and the US Navy is building more 'Lightning Carriers' to embark US Marine Corps jets. Turkey has announced proposals for next generation carriers. Spain is looking to buy new jets for its flat top.

Naval technology moves quickly. Just as jet powered aircraft replaced propeller aircraft after World War Two, naval aviation is on the verge of a new revolution. Unmanned aerial vehicles or drones as they are more popularly known, are starting to arrive on carrier decks. Britain and the United States have experimented with flying large drones off the decks of their carriers for strike, air-to-air »

ABOVE: Navies around the world continue to invest in new aircraft carriers because of their intrinsic flexibility. The new USS *John F Kennedy* is under construction and her price tag of more than $12 billion is making even the US Navy blanch. (US NAVY)

LEFT: Boeing's unmanned MQ-25 aerial refuelling tanker has flown experimental missions from the USS *George HW Bush*. (US NAVY)

LEFT: The Northrop Grumman X-47B Unmanned Combat Air System (UCAS) demonstrator carried out flight trials from the USS *George HW Bush* in 2013. (US NAVY)

ABOVE: France's PAAG carrier is expected to the replace the *FS Charles de Gaulle* in 2040 it has been proposed that she have an air wing of manned and unmanned aircraft. (RAMA)

refuelling, airborne early warning, and cargo delivery.

Turkey has declared it is going to leapfrog operating manned fast jets from its new carrier and is going to start operating strike and reconnaissance drones from its newly commissioned flat top. The era of drone carriers could be here very soon.

Drone carriers could transform how carrier aviation operates. Swarms of attack drones could be launched to overwhelm defences. Air refuelling would allow drones swarms to stay on stay on task for far longer than manned aircraft, which are limited by the endurance of their human pilots or crews. Aircraft carriers can

potentially embark far more drones that manned aircraft. They can be stored in boxes when not being used and they require a fraction of the maintenance compared to manned aircraft. The biggest difference is that naval air commanders no longer have to be worried about losing human aviators to enemy action. Drone pilots cannot be taken prisoner and paraded on television for propaganda value. This new paradigm means that naval air warfare could potentially involving hundreds of drones – both friendly and hostile – being in the air at the same time, making naval air battles more confusing and deadly. This could see a return to those classic carrier battles

of World War Two, where the rival air armadas struck at each other carriers.

The aircraft carrier is the ultimate high value asset and hostile navies continue to put huge efforts into trying to kill them. Sea skimming missiles of the Cold War era have been augmented today by anti-ship ballistic and hypersonic missiles threatening to overwhelm the air defences of carrier battle groups.

The recent confrontation in the Red Sea has seen carrier fleet air defence come to the fore, with fighters, missiles and close-in gun defences having to be combined to defeat Houthi drones and ballistic missiles. The ability of the carrier air power to rapidly strike back to hit land targets has proved instrumental to US and coalition operations, to keep the pressure on Houthi forces and stop them massing to attack shipping in the Red Sea. This operation has been described as the most intense period of US Navy carrier combat operations since World War Two, with the coalition warships simultaneous engaging incoming Houthi drones and missiles, while at the same time striking back at land targets.

Carrier-based airpower has provided coalition commanders with the ability to rapidly react to Houthi threats and at the same time co-ordinate fleet wide defence operations. The USS *Dwight D Eisenhower* and her battlegroup dominated the Red Sea and showed that carrier air power could still cut it in a 21st century naval battle.

RIGHT: Bayraktar Kızılelma combat drones are being developed to operate off the Turkish Navy's assault ship, the TCG *Anadolu*. (ATA BARIS)